1000 FACTS ON
OCEANS

First published by Bardfield Press in 2005
Copyright © 2005 Miles Kelly Publishing Ltd

Bardfield Press is an imprint of
Miles Kelly Publishing Ltd,
Bardfield Centre, Great Bardfield, Essex, CM7 4SL

Some of the material also appears in *Visual Factfinder Oceans*

2 4 6 8 10 9 7 5 3 1

Editorial Director
Belinda Gallagher

Copy Editor
Stuart Cooper

Editorial Assistant
Amanda Askew

Picture Researcher
Liberty Newton

Designer
Tom Slemmings

Production Manager
Estela Boulton

Scanning and reprographics
Anthony Cambray, Mike Coupe, Ian Paulyn

British Library Cataloguing-in-Publication Data
A catalogue record for this book is available from the British Library

ISBN 1-84236-554-1

Printed in China

www.mileskelly.net
info@mileskelly.net

1000 FACTS ON
OCEANS

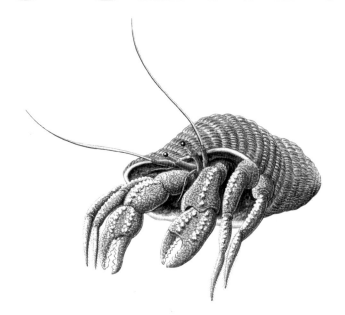

Consultant: Clint Twist

BARDFIELD PRESS

Contents

Key

 Sea and coast

 Marine fish

 Mammals, birds and reptiles

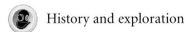 History and exploration

 Ships and boats

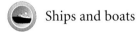 Human impact

Contents

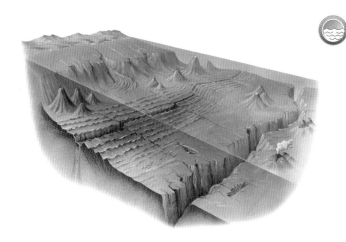

The blue planet 8, Oceans of the world 10, Studying the oceans 12, Ocean floor 14, Trenches and ridges 16, Causing waves 18, Coastlines 20, Sea caves 22, Volcanic oceans 24, Volcanic islands 26, The angry oceans 28, Coral reefs 30, Amazing corals 32, Icy water 34, The Arctic 36, Antarctica 38, Glaciers and icebergs 40

Early marine life 42, Modern marine life 44, Fish facts 46, Flying fish 48, Herring 50, Tuna and mackerel 52, Swordfish 54, Barracuda 56, Eels 58, Seahorses 60, Sharks 62, Incredible hunters 64, Great white shark 66, Hammerhead shark 68, Whale shark 70, Rays 72

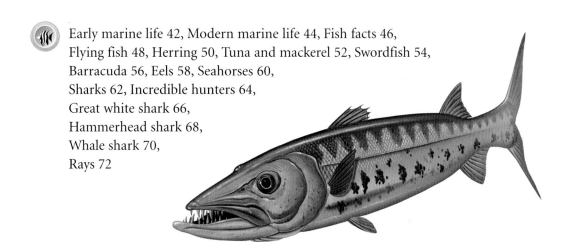

Contents

Whales 74, Baleen and blubber 76, Blue whale 78,
Killer whale 80, Humpback whale 82, Beluga 84,
Dolphins 86, Porpoises 88, Seals 90, Sea lions 92,
Sea cows 94, Gulls 96, Albatrosses 98, Pelicans 100,
Penguins 102, Sea turtles 104, Sea snakes 106

The first boats 108, Ancient cargo ships 110,
The ancient Greek navy 112, The ancient
Roman navy 114, Viking voyagers 116,
Christopher Columbus 118, Vasco da Gama 120,
Ferdinand Magellan 122, Sir Francis Drake 124,
The Spanish Armada 126, Pirate aboard! 128,
Voyages to Australia 130, Napoleon versus
Nelson 132, The *Titanic* 134, Finding the way 136,
Diving through time 138, Underwater fashion 140

Ships today 142, Modern navigation 144, Modern cargo ships 146, Tankers 148, Container ships 150, Fishing vessels 152, Luxurious liners 154, Ferries 156, Tugs and icebreakers 158, Submersibles and tenders 160, Battleships 162, Aircraft carriers 164, Submarines 166, Rowing boats 168, Sailing ships 170, Surfing 172, Powered for fun 174, Riding the waves 176

Oceans in danger 178, Greenhouse effect 180, Sinking lands 182, Bleaching the reefs 184, Mineral rich 186, Fossil fuels 188, Drilling for oil 190, Oil spills 192, Ocean pollution 194, Cleaning the oceans 196, Saving ocean life 198, Endangered species 200, Whaling and fishing 202, Crowding the coasts 204, Living at sea 206

The blue planet

- **The Earth** is the only planet in the Solar System with enough oxygen and water to support life. However, it was not always so. At first the Earth had no oxygen or atmosphere. Only traces of hydrogen and helium were present.

- **When it first formed**, the Earth was continuously being hit by rocks and other materials from space. These collisions generated immense heat, causing rocks to melt.

- **At the same time**, radioactive elements on the Earth also released a lot of heat, causing heavier elements such as iron and nickel to sink deep into the centre of the Earth to form its core. Lighter elements such as silicon floated to the surface.

- **The layer** surrounding the core is called the mantle, which is in a partially molten state. The mantle comprises the bulk of the Earth's weight and volume.

- **About 4 billion years ago** the Earth's surface cooled and solidified to form the topmost layer, called the crust. The crust was broken into several rock fragments, called tectonic plates, that floated on the mantle.

- **These plates** moved past each other, often colliding and causing friction. This collision built up pressure beneath the crust, leading to volcanic eruptions that caused cracks on the Earth's surface.

> ...FASCINATING FACT...
> Acids in the rainwater corroded the rocks on the Earth's surface.
> Chemicals in these rocks were carried into the oceans. Among these
> chemicals were certain salts that made the ocean water salty.

- **Gases**, such as hydrogen and nitrogen, and water vapour burst through the cracks in the crust. These constant eruptions slowly led to the formation of the atmosphere.

- **Water vapour** condensed to form clouds that enveloped the Earth and eventually brought rain. However, the Earth's surface was so hot that the rainwater evaporated immediately.

- **As the rains** continued the Earth started to cool and the volcanic activity decreased. Water poured down for thousands of years to fill up huge pits and form oceans.

- **The rain** also formed smaller bodies of water such as rivers and lakes. At high altitudes, the water froze and fell as snow. The snow melted and flowed down mountains as streams and rivers.

▶ *Volcanoes continuously erupted, covering the surface of the primeval Earth with oceans of lava, making it unfit for life.*

9

Oceans of the world

- **Oceans cover** almost 362 million sq km of the Earth's surface. Although there is only one ocean that covers the world, it has been divided into four major ocean basins. A fifth ocean, the Antarctic Ocean, also called the Southern Ocean, was recently added to this list.

- **The four basins** are the Pacific, Atlantic, Indian and Arctic oceans. The Arctic Ocean surrounds the North Pole and is largely frozen.

- **The Antarctic Ocean** is actually formed by the southern extensions of the Pacific, Atlantic and Indian oceans. Hence this ocean was, for a long time, not considered as a separate entity.

- **The international dispute** regarding the status of the Antarctic Ocean continued until the year 2000. The International Hydrographic Organization has since recognized the waters surrounding Antarctica as the fifth ocean and named it the Southern Ocean.

- **The Pacific Ocean** is the largest of all oceans. At 166 million sq km, it is twice the size of the Atlantic Ocean. The Pacific Ocean's average depth is more than 4000 m, making it the world's deepest ocean.

- **This ocean** gets its name from the Spanish word *pacifico*, which means peaceful. During his voyage around the world, Portuguese explorer Ferdinand Magellan found the Pacific to be calm and hence gave the ocean its name.

- **The Atlantic Ocean**, at 82 million sq km, is the second largest ocean. It is also the stormiest. The most interesting feature of this ocean is the mid-ocean ridge that runs through its entire length.

- **This ocean** contains some of the most important seas and other features. These include the Baltic Sea, Black Sea, Caribbean Sea, Mediterranean Sea, Gulf of Mexico, Labrador Sea, Denmark Strait and Norwegian Sea.

- **The Indian Ocean** has a total area of over 73 million sq km. It is bounded by the three continents of Asia, Africa and Oceania. Some of the earliest known civilizations, such as the Mesopotamian, Egyptian and Indus Valley civilizations, developed near this ocean.

- **The Arctic Ocean**, at 14 million sq km, is the smallest among the world's oceans. It is also the shallowest. The deepest point in the Arctic Ocean is only 5450 m – not even half as deep as the deepest point of the Pacific Ocean.

▼ *The Pacific Ocean is deep enough to engulf the whole of Mount Everest without trace.*

Studying the oceans

- **The study** of the chemical and physical properties of oceans and their ecosystems is called oceanography, oceanology or marine science.

- **Oceanography** comprises marine geology, physical oceanography, chemical oceanography, marine biology and meteorological oceanography.

▲ *A satellite photograph of a hurricane forming over the Earth. Meteorological oceanography deals with the influence of oceans on weather patterns across the world.*

- **Marine geology** deals with the study of tectonic plates in the Earth's crust. These plates are responsible for natural phenomena such as volcanoes, earthquakes, mountains and valleys.

- **Apart from studying** the Earth's crust and other related phenomena, marine geologists involved in offshore oil exploration and drilling also study how sediments and minerals are formed.

- **Physical oceanography** is the study of the physical processes that take place in the oceans. These include ocean currents, temperature, salt content in ocean water and the causes of tides.

- **Chemical oceanography** is the study of chemicals in the oceans. The seas contain most of the elements found in the Earth, including fossil fuels and minerals.

- **Oceanography** also includes allied sciences such as the study of caves, or speleology. This subject deals with the origin, physical structure and development of caves. It also studies the flora and fauna of caves.

- **Hydrography** is another important branch of oceanography. It is the oldest science that deals with the sea and is defined as the study of water depth and quality, and of material found on the ocean floor, with specific reference to their impact on navigation.

- **Oceanography** gained importance with the age of discovery in AD1400–1500. New lands were being discovered and oceans were mapped out during this time by explorers from great maritime nations such as Portugal and Spain.

- **Meteorological oceanography** deals with the interaction between the oceans and the atmosphere. It is the study of atmospheric reactions above the oceans and the influence of the oceans on global weather.

Ocean floor

- **The Earth's surface** is covered by the oceans and seven huge land masses, called continents. Oceans cover about 71 percent of our planet's surface.

- **At certain places** the land rises above the water to form continents and islands. The surface under the oceans is called the ocean floor.

- **The ocean floor** is broadly divided into the continental shelf, the continental slope and deep ocean floor.

- **The continental shelf** is an underwater extension of the coast. The rim of islands and continents gently slopes into the surrounding water to form the continental shelf.

- **The average width** of the continental shelf is about 65 km but some, such as the Siberian Shelf in the Arctic Ocean, can extend up to 1500 km.

- **The continental shelf** is commercially very important. It contains large deposits of petroleum, natural gas and minerals. This area also receives the most sunlight and marine life thrives here.

- **The continental slope** is the point where the shelf starts to plunge steeply towards the ocean floor. Here the ocean floor is marked by deep canyons.

- **Below continental slopes** sediments often collect to form gentle slopes called continental rise. The continental shelf, slope and rise are together known as continental margin.

- **In many places** the ocean floor forms vast expanses that are flat and covered with sediment. These regions are called the abyssal plains.

- **The abyssal plain** is broken by mid-ocean ridges, such as the Mid-Atlantic and the East Pacific rise, and trenches such as the Mariana Trench in the Pacific Ocean.

▼ *Beneath the oceans is a landscape similar to that found on land.*

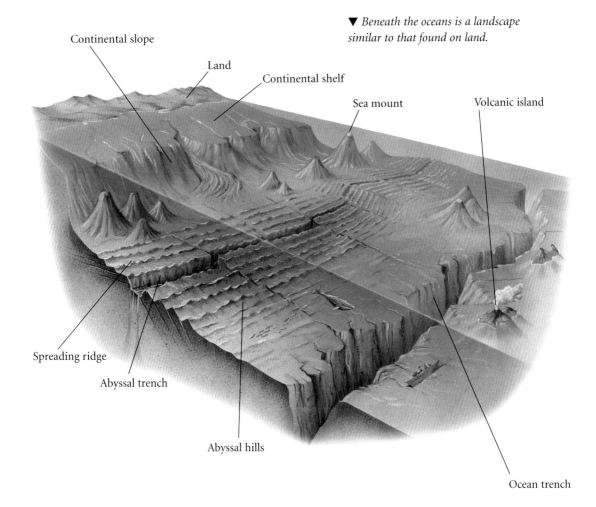

Continental slope

Land

Continental shelf

Sea mount

Volcanic island

Spreading ridge

Abyssal trench

Abyssal hills

Ocean trench

15

Trenches and ridges

- **The ocean floor**, like land, has high mountains, deep valleys, canyons and vast plains.

- **The most dramatic** of the ocean floor structures are the trenches, or deep valleys, and ridges, or mountain chains.

- **The Earth's crust** is made up of several huge, flat rock segments called tectonic plates. These plates slide and move against each other.

- **The movement** of these plates is responsible for the formation of ridges and trenches.

- **Ridges are formed** when two plates drift apart. Hot lava oozes out through the cracks and cools to form a ridge. A trench is formed when the heavier plate plunges beneath the lighter one.

- **Mariana Trench** is one of the deepest trenches. It is located in the Pacific Ocean, to the east of the Philippines.

- **The Challenger Deep**, in the Mariana Trench, is the deepest point in the Earth. At 11,033 m its depth is more than the height of Mount Everest.

- **The mid-ocean ridge** is the longest mountain chain on Earth. It is over 50,000 km long. The crests of these mountains lie nearly 2500 m below the ocean surface.

- **At some places** the mid-ocean ridge is exposed above the sea level. Iceland is located on top of one such crest of the mid-Atlantic ocean ridge.

- **Seamounts are** underwater volcanoes. A flat-topped seamount is known as a guyot, while those with peaks are known as seapeaks.

▲ *On January 23, 1960, US Navy Leiutenant Don Walsh and Swiss scientist, Jacques Piccard, set a record by descending to the bottom of the Challenger Deep, in the US Navy submersible,* Trieste.

Causing waves

- **Oceans** are never completely at rest. They are rocked by several kinds of movements, such as waves, currents and tides.

- **Most movements** in the oceans, such as waves and surface currents, are caused by wind. Waves are created by winds blowing over the surface of the oceans. The stronger the wind, the larger the waves.

- **The water in a wave moves** in circles and not forward as it may appear. As a wave nears land it slows down because of the shallower seabed. The top part of the wave carries on and crashes on the shore as a breaker.

- **The shape and size** of waves differ. A steep, choppy wave is one that has just been formed near the coast, while the slow, steady ones are those that originated far out in the ocean.

- **The regular rise and fall** of the oceans are called tides. They are caused by the gravitational pull of the Sun and the Moon. Since the Moon is closer to the Earth, its effect is felt more.

- **The period** of high water level is known as high tide and the period of low water level is known as low tide.

- **An ocean current** is a mass of water moving continuously in one direction. Surface currents are caused by winds and rotation of the Earth, while differences in temperature and salt content are responsible for underwater currents.

- **Most ocean currents** flow in large loops called gyres, which spin clockwise in the Northern Hemisphere and anti-clockwise in the Southern Hemisphere. This is due to the Earth's rotation and is called the Coriolis Effect.

● **When the Sun, Moon and Earth** are in a straight line their combined gravities cause unusually high tides, called spring tides. This alignment of the three happens during full Moon and new Moon. Smaller tides, called neap tides, occur at other times when the Moon is at a right angle to the Sun and the Earth.

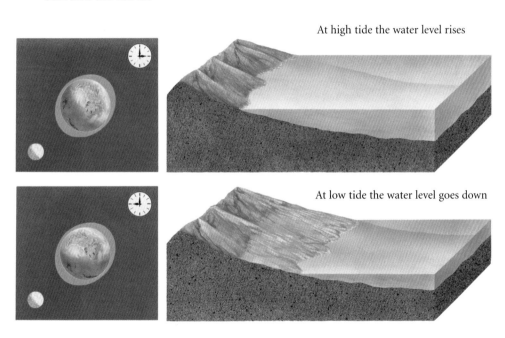

At high tide the water level rises

At low tide the water level goes down

▲ *High tide happens on those parts of the Earth that are closest to and farthest away from the Moon. As the Earth turns, approximately six hours later, the water subsides. This is called the low tide.*

19

Coastlines

- **A coast** is a continuous stretch of land that borders an ocean. It is made up of sand, mud and gravel. The outline of the coast is called a coastline.

- **The features** of a coast depend on the wind, rocks and currents in that area. Strong winds whip up equally strong waves that pound the rocks on the coastlines and erode them.

- **Hard rocks** are able to withstand the pounding of waves and erode slowly, forming headlands.

- **Wave power** is also responsible for the formation of structures such as cliffs, headlands, sea caves, sea arches, sea stacks and beach heads.

- **A cliff** is formed by the constant pounding of waves on weak spots on the rock face. At first, a tiny gap is created. This gap enlarges as the rock continues to erode, eventually causing its roof to collapse.

- **When softer rocks** at the base of a cliff erode first, they collapse on to the shore. They break into minute fragments, eventually forming wide beaches between the existing cliff and the ocean. This saves the cliff from further erosion.

- **Continuous erosion** leads to the creation of hollows, called sea caves, in the headlands. Sometimes waves pound the headland from either side, causing caves to form on both sides of the headland.

> ...FASCINATING FACT...
> Long Beach is the world's longest beach. It is located along the southwest coast of Washington, the capital of the United States. This beach stretches for a record 45 km.

- **When two back-to-back caves** meet, a sea arch is formed. The top portion of the arch links the headland to the mainland like a bridge.

- **After years of erosion**, the sea arches cave in. This leaves only a column of rock standing independently in the sea. This is known as a sea stack.

- **The best-known** natural structure formed by the action of waves is the beach. Waves lose much of their power in shallow waters and instead of eroding they start depositing sand and shingle, carried into the oceans by rivers, on the coast. These deposits eventually become the beach.

▶ *Waves can create amazing shapes such as pillars called sea stacks.*

Sea stack

Sea arch

Sea caves

- **Sea caves** are formed when the force of the waves wears away rocks situated at the base of cliffs.

- **These rocks** are usually weak due to a fault or fracture in them. Even vein-like cracks are enough to cause rocks to crumble under continuous pounding by huge waves.

- **Waves penetrate** cracks in a rock and exert high pressure, forcing the rocks to crumble from within, forming small hollows.

- **These hollows** expand further when sand, gravel and rocks brought by the waves start eroding the inner walls of the rocks.

- **Some sea caves** are submerged in water during high tide, and can be seen only when the water recedes.

- **Sea caves** are a great attraction for adventurers and tourists. They can be explored in small boats or on foot when the water level is low.

- **Sea caves** are common on the Pacific coasts of the United States and in the Greek islands. The Blue Grotto of Capri in Italy is famous for the bluish glow of its waters. This glow is caused by sunlight pouring through an underwater hole. The light shines on the water to create a brilliant blue glow.

- **Sea caves are full of** marine life. Sea anemones, sponges and starfish are found in the bigger caves.

> **...FASCINATING FACT...**
> One of the largest known sea caves is the Painted Cave on Santa Cruz Island off California. It is nearly 375 m long. The cave gets its name from the colourful patterns on the rocks.

▲ *Sea caves on the island of Cyprus. Caves can be of various sizes. Some may extend hundreds of metres into the rock and have more than one tunnel.*

23

Volcanic oceans

- **Almost 90 percent** of the world's volcanic activity takes place under the ocean. Most undersea volcanoes are along the mid-ocean ridge.

- **The Pacific Ocean** contains more than 80 percent of the world's active volcanoes. These volcanoes encircle the ocean along the continent margins to form the 'Ring of Fire'.

- **Volcanoes** are formed when two tectonic plates drift apart and hot molten rock called magma oozes out. They are also formed if one plate crashes into another.

- **When the lava** oozing out of an underwater volcano comes into contact with water, it solidifies quickly. This lava often forms round lumps called pillow lava. Several tiny marine organisms thrive on these lumps of lava.

- **Underwater volcanic mountains** are known as seamounts. Some seamounts, called guyots, are extinct volcanoes with flat tops. Some guyots could also have been volcanic islands that were eroded with time.

- **Hot springs,** or hydrothermal vents, are also found on the sea floor along the mid-ocean ridge. They are formed when water seeps into the crust as two plates pull apart. This water is heated by the magma and shoots up through cracks in the ocean floor.

> ...FASCINATING FACT...
> Mauna Kea and Mauna Loa in Hawaii are the tallest volcanic
> mountains on Earth. Measured from its base on the ocean floor,
> Mauna Kea at 9800 m is taller than even Mount Everest.

▲ *Hydrothermal vents are home to rat tail fish and sea spiders as well as giant tube worms.*

- **The temperature** of water in and around a vent can go up to 400°C. This water is rich in minerals and the gas hydrogen sulphide.

- **The scalding water** mixes with the surrounding cold water to create chimney-like jets of warm water. These jets are often black because of the mineral content in the water. Hence hydrothermal vents are also called black smokers.

- **Hydrothermal vents** were first discovered in 1977 near the Galapagos Islands along the eastern Pacific Ocean basin. Scientists travelling in the submersible *ALVIN* observed these vents about 2500 m below the ocean's surface.

- **The water** at the deep-ocean floor is too cold for creatures to survive, but hydrothermal vents are like underwater oases. Long tubeworms and other life forms that are not found anywhere else in the world thrive near these vents.

25

Volcanic islands

- **Undersea volcanoes** often lead to the formation of volcanic islands. Some of these islands are formed around one or two volcanic vents, while others can be made up of a series of vents.

- **Volcanic activity** usually occurs at the point where two tectonic plates meet or break away. Sometimes, volcanoes are formed away from the plate boundaries near areas called hot spots, which are fixed points of volcanic activity located beneath the tectonic plates.

- **Molten magma** from deep within the mantle forces its way through fissures (gaps) in the plate and flow out to form seamounts.

- **Over millions of years** magma keeps oozing out of these seamounts, which gradually rise above the ocean surface as islands. These islands are called oceanic high islands.

- **The constant movement** of tectonic plates eventually carries an island away from the hot spot and volcanic activity ceases in that island. Meanwhile, another island is created near the hot spot. This continues until a chain of islands, such as the Hawaiian Islands, is created.

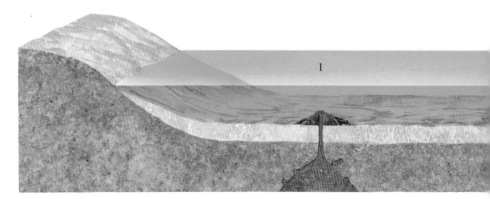

- **The hot spot** in the Pacific Ocean is currently under the Big Island, which is the largest among the Hawaiian Islands.

- **The Big Island** has five volcanoes. They are Kilauea, Mauna Loa, Mauna Kea, Hualalai and Kohala. Kilauea is the most active volcano in the region.

- **Iceland was formed** by volcano activity near the ocean ridge. It is the only part of the mid-oceanic ridge that emerges from the surface.

- **Some volcanic islands** are formed in the shape of arcs, such as Marianas and the Aleutian Islands in the Pacific Ocean.

- **Island arcs** form when one plate slides below the other. The magma oozes out, forming volcanoes on the edge of the plate above. These volcanoes eventually emerge from the ocean surface as islands in the shape of an arc.

▼ *When volcanoes erupt under the sea, new islands may appear.*
(1) Molten rock breaks through Earth's crust . (2) As more lava is deposited on the seabed, a cone shape builds up. (3) When this breaks the water's surface, a new island appears. The volcano may go on erupting.

The angry oceans

- **The oceans**, which are a source of invaluable resources, can also wreak havoc in the form of tsunamis, whirlpools and hurricanes.

- **There are times when** a series of massive waves are generated in the oceans by certain natural disturbances. These waves, called tsunamis, lash against the shore with such great force that they cause a lot of damage.

- **Tsunamis** are most often created by earthquakes. They can also be generated by landslides and undersea volcanic eruptions, and are often incorrectly referred to as tidal waves.

- **Most tsunamis** originate along a volcanic and earthquake-prone zone known as the Ring of Fire, around the Pacific Ocean. Tsunami is a Japanese word meaning 'harbour wave'.

- **Hurricanes** are violent tropical cyclones arising in the tropical or sub-tropical waters. Hurricanes of the northwest Pacific Ocean are called typhoons.

- **The strongest and most dangerous hurricanes** are classified as Category 5. These hurricanes are rare, and the wind speed exceeds 250 km/h.

...FASCINATING FACT...
El Niño was first observed by fishermen in South America, who noticed that this phenomenon usually occurred near the time of Christmas. Hence, they named it El Niño, meaning 'the infant' in Spanish.

▶ *Hurricanes form over the Atlantic Ocean and move westward through the Caribbean and across the southern United States. These storms can cause devastation if they reach the coast.*

- **A whirlpool is** created when opposing currents or tides meet in the ocean. The uneven ocean floor makes the water swirl in with great force. Most whirlpools are not dangerous. However, some are powerful enough to destroy small boats.

- **Mosktraumen** off the coast of Norway and Old Sow near Deer Island in Canada are two of the world's most powerful whirlpools.

- **El Niño** is another interesting oceanic phenomenon that has a considerable effect on the global weather. It is the warming of surface waters in the eastern Pacific Ocean, near the Equator.

- **El Niño** causes an increase in rainfall across the southern states of the United States and in parts of South America. This usually leads to destructive floods in these regions. It is also believed to be responsible for drought in Africa and Australia.

Coral reefs

- **Coral reefs** are formed by colonies of coral polyps. A coral polyp is a tiny animal that uses minerals in the sea to produce a protective outer skeleton. These skeletons form hard and branching structures called coral reefs.

- **Coral polyps** eat algae. They also use their tentacles to capture tiny creatures called zooplankton.

- **Corals** are ancient animals that have been around for 250 millions years.

- **Coral reefs** are home to numerous sea animals. Starfish, reef sharks, sponges, jellyfish, crabs, lobsters, anemones, eels and a huge variety of fish add to the colour of coral reefs.

- **Coral reefs are found** in warm and shallow waters, usually within 30 degrees north and south of the Equator.

- **There are three kinds** of coral reefs. These are fringing and barrier reefs, and coral atolls.

- **Fringing reefs** extend from the land into the sea. Barrier reefs are found further from the shore, separated from the mainland by a lagoon. Atolls are ring-shaped formations of coral islands, around a lagoon.

- **The Great Barrier Reef** in the Coral Sea off the north-eastern coast of Australia is the biggest of all coral reefs. It is over 2000 km long.

- **Coral reefs** are also found in the Indian Ocean and the Red Sea. Some of them also stretch along the Atlantic Ocean from Florida in the United States to the Caribbean Sea and Brazil.

- **Coral reefs**, especially the Great Barrier Reef, are major tourist attractions because of their fascinating structures, vibrant colours and rich marine life.

...FASCINATING FACT...
The stinging hydroid coral found in the Indian and
Pacific oceans uses special chemicals to paralyse
plankton, which forms a major part of its diet.

▼ *A single coral reef may be home to as many as 3000 species of living things.*

Amazing corals

▲ *Coral reefs, which support a wide variety of marine life, are the largest ecosystems on our planet.*

- **An atoll** is a low-lying coral island consisting of a coral reef surrounding a lagoon. There are several stages in the formation of an atoll and it could take millions of years for the island to emerge.

- **The first stage** of atoll formation includes the creation of a coral reef around a volcanic island. Strong winds and waves slowly erode the island and it begins to sink. But the reef continues to grow upwards to form a barrier reef separated from the sinking island by a lagoon. At this stage these islands are called barrier reef islands.

- **The barrier reef islands** continue to sink until the land is completely submerged. However, the reef around the island continues to grow upwards to form a ring surrounding a lagoon. This is called a coral atoll.

- **Coral atolls** are formed mostly in warm and shallow waters of the Indian and Pacific oceans. Marshall, Tuamotu and Kiribati islands are atoll chains in the Pacific Ocean.

- **Sometimes, waves and wind** deposit small pieces of coral and sand on top of reefs. Over thousands of years, this debris piles up to form low-lying islands called cays.

- **Coral cays** are known to support a variety of plant and animal life. Some cays eventually become small islands that people live on. However, other cays move across the reef and even disappear with time.

- **Kiritimati**, or Christmas Island, is the largest coral atoll in the world. It is one of the Line Islands, a group of islands belonging to the Republic of Kiribati, which comprises 32 low-lying atolls and one raised island.

- **Three of the four atolls** in the Caribbean Sea can be found off the coast of Belize, near Mexico. They are the Turneffe Atoll, Glover's Reef and Lighthouse Reef.

- **The Belize atolls** are unique. Unlike other atolls, these did not grow around volcanic islands. Instead, they developed on non-volcanic ridges.

- **The Coral Sea Islands**, off the east coast of Australia, is one of the smallest countries in the world. It comprises numerous small uninhabited coral reefs and cays spread over a sea area of about 780,000 sq km.

- **The colourful reefs** that surround coral islands are home to beautiful and exotic marine creatures. These reefs have become popular destinations for undersea diving.

Icy water

- **The oceans** close to the North and South poles – the Arctic and the Antarctic – are partly frozen throughout the year.

- **These oceans** are covered with dazzling white icebergs and huge sheets of floating ice, which make it difficult for ships to navigate these waters.

- **The Antarctic Ocean** surrounds Antarctica, which is an island continent. The Arctic Ocean surrounds the North Pole.

- **In winter** the water close to the land is frozen. The ice melts in the summer and large chunks of ice, called icebergs, break off and float in the sea.

- **Massive slabs** of permanent ice, or ice shelves, break off and also float close to the shores in the Antarctic Ocean. The Ross Ice Shelf is the largest of these.

- **Unlike the South Pole**, there is no land mass around the North Pole. Most parts of the Arctic Ocean are covered by ice sheets.

- **Apart from the Arctic** and Antarctic oceans, there are other seas that freeze during winter. The Okhotsk Sea and the Bering Sea, divided by the Kamchatka Peninsula in the north-western Pacific region, remain frozen during the winter.

- **The water** in the Polar Regions might be freezing cold, but it is still home to a wide range of marine life. Whales, sharks, jellyfish, squid, seals, polar bears and seabirds can be found living in and around these oceans.

- **The harsh climate** on the Antarctic continent, however, is not conducive to life. This region is largely uninhabited. Only scientists brave the cold to conduct research. However, Inuit are known to live in the Arctic region.

◀ *The term 'iceberg' has its origin in the German word* berg, *meaning mountain.*

The Arctic – a profile

- **The Arctic region** is not a clearly defined area. All of the Earth that falls inside the Arctic Circle is termed as 'the Arctic'. The Arctic Circle is the imaginary circle surrounding the North Pole. Unlike Antarctica, it is not a single land mass or continent.

- **The North Pole** is in the middle of the Arctic Ocean. The ocean is surrounded by Russia, Greenland, Iceland, Canada and Alaska.

- **Contrary to popular belief**, the North Pole is not the coldest part of the Arctic region. Oymyakon in Siberia is actually the coldest, with a temperature of –68°C.

- **A large part of the land** surrounding the Arctic Ocean is extremely cold and treeless. This region is called the tundra. The word tundra is from the Finnish word *tunturia*, which means barren land.

- **The Arctic tundra** is so cold that the ground beneath the surface remains frozen throughout the year. This frozen ground is called permafrost. The topmost layer of the permafrost thaws every summer.

▼ *Snowmobiles have replaced dog sledges as a popular mode of transport in the Arctic region.*

- **The permafrost** does not allow plants to grow deep roots. Hence, the tundra is not suitable for trees. However, a large variety of mosses, lichens, shrubs and small flowering plants can be found in this region.

- **The Arctic is home** to animals and birds such as the Arctic fox, seals, orcas, beluga whales, Greenland sharks, polar bears and caribou. However, not all creatures live in the region throughout the year. A lot of mammals and birds are seen only during the summer.

- **Inuit**, or Eskimos, are the original inhabitants of the Arctic region. The word 'Eskimo' means 'eater of raw meat' in Algonquian, a Native American language. Today these people prefer to be called 'Inuit', which means 'the people' in the language Inuktitut.

- **Traditionally the Inuit** depended mostly on seals for their survival as the meat provided food, while the blubber was used as fuel and to make tents. During summer they travelled in boats made from animal skin, called kayaks. In winter they used dog sledges.

- **Today most Inuit live** in houses made of wood instead of igloos or tents. They wear modern clothing and travel in motorboats and snowmobiles. They also speak English, Russian or Danish apart from their native tongue.

> **...FASCINATING FACT...**
> The Earth revolves around the Sun on a tilted axis. This means the North Pole faces the Sun during the summer and faces away from the Sun in the winter. As a result, in summer the North Pole has sunshine all day long, even at midnight, but in winter it is in total darkness all day, even at midday.

Antarctica – a profile

- **Antarctica** is the fifth largest continent. It lies in the southernmost point of the globe, and surrounds the South Pole.

- **It is an island** continent, surrounded by the icy Antarctic Ocean. The total area is about 14 million sq km in summer. This is almost 50 times the size of the United Kingdom.

- **Antarctica** is roughly round in shape. Two seas, Weddell Sea to the northwest and the Ross Sea to the southwest, cut into the continent.

- **Antarctica** was the last continent to be discovered. It is the remotest land mass, and by far the coldest and the windiest.

- **This continent** has the lowest temperatures on Earth. During winter, the temperature falls below –90 °C.

- **Antarctica** receives no rainfall. It is often referred to as a cold desert. The snow hardly melts or evaporates. Instead, it accumulates in icy layers.

- **The thick ice cover** makes Antarctica the highest of all continents, with an average height of about 2300 m. The ice covering this continent makes up 70 percent of the Earth's fresh water.

- **The continent** has been broadly divided into Greater Antarctica and West Antarctica. Both these areas are separated by the Transantarctic Mountains. A large portion of this mountain range is buried under ice.

> **...FASCINATING FACT...**
> The Antarctic Treaty (1961) allows only peaceful activities such as scientific research on the continent and its ocean.

● **At certain places** taller parts of the Transantarctic Mountains manage to peek out of the ice. These tips of rocks, called *nunatak*, are often home to birds, such as snow petrels.

▼ *Antarctica has been covered with ice for about five million years. It is home to large colonies of penguins.*

Glaciers and icebergs

▲ *The process by which icebergs break away from glaciers is called 'calving'. Icebergs are said to make a fizzing sound when they calve.*

- **Glaciers** are moving masses of ice. They form on top of high mountains and in the polar regions, where temperatures are well below freezing point during winter and the summer is not warm enough to melt the snow.

- **Continuous snowfall** leads to the accumulation of snow. Each year, new layers of snow compress the previous layers, gradually forming ice.

- **Once the glacier** attains enough weight, it slowly starts sliding down a slope. Glaciers can be broadly divided into four types depending upon where they were formed. These are icecap, alpine, piedmont and continental glaciers.

- **Alpine glaciers** originate from mountains and feed mountain rivers. Piedmont glaciers are formed when alpine glaciers join at the foot of a mountain.

- **A huge blanket** of ice and snow covers most of Greenland and Antarctica. These formations are known as continental glaciers, or ice sheets.

- **Icecap glaciers** are miniature versions of continental glaciers. They usually occupy elevated regions such as plateau. Sometimes these icecaps break off at the edges and fall into the ocean.

- **Icebergs** are massive chunks of ice that break off the ends of ice sheets, glaciers and ice caps and then float into the sea.

- **The largest icebergs** are formed from ice shelves. These shelves crack at the outer ends, and icebergs drift into the sea.

- **The ice in some icebergs** contains tiny air bubbles that reflect light and give the iceberg a dazzling, white look. Ice that melts and freezes again can give the iceberg a blue tint.

- **Icebergs** are different shapes and sizes. They can be broadly classified as rounded, irregular and tabular, or resembling a table top.

> ...FASCINATING FACT...
> The part of an iceberg that is visible above water is only a
> small portion of its entire bulk. The enormous submerged
> part can cause great danger to ships. The saying 'tip of the
> iceberg' has its origins in this phenomenon.

Early marine life

- **It is believed** that life on Earth originated in the oceans around 3.8 billion years ago.

- **According to some scientists**, repeated lightning strikes triggered a reaction among certain compounds and gases in the Earth's atmosphere. This reaction might have led to the formation of proteins and enzymes, which are the building blocks of life.

- **The proteins and enzymes** rained down on the oceans and developed into primitive single-celled organisms.

- **Around 620 million years ago**, complex and soft-bodied multi-cellular life-forms appeared for the first time.

- **Some of the earliest creatures** looked like modern jellyfish. They were very small and had a variety of shapes.

- **These early animals** soon evolved into more complex life-forms that are recognized today. Some of these early creatures included sponges, jellyfish, corals, flatworms and molluscs.

- **The earliest fish** appeared around 480 million years ago. These were the jawless fish. The modern hagfish and lamprey are the only surviving members of this group.

- **Around 450 million years ago**, sharks and bony fish began to evolve. The first bony fish were small and had armoured plates for defence.

- **The early bony fish** were either ray-finned or lobe-finned. The coelacanth and the modern lungfish are the only lobe-finned fish that survive today.

- **Most scientists** believe that lobe-finned fish used their fins to come out of the water for very short periods. This led to the evolution of amphibians, which themselves eventually evolved into other land creatures.

▲ *Coelacanths are referred to as 'living fossils' because they have changed very little over millions of years.*

Modern marine life

- **The first modern fish** appeared around 250 million years ago. The ancient ray-finned fish gave rise to the neopterygians, which are considered to be the ancestors of the modern fish.

- **The oceans** of the modern world are no different from the primitive oceans in terms of the number of creatures that live there. Today, the oceans are home to several species of mammals and reptiles, numerous small creatures and more than 20,000 species of fish.

- **Oceans** are divided into two regions – the benthic zone, or the ocean floor, and the pelagic zone, which is the vast expanse of water.

- **The pelagic zone** is further divided into three zones. The topmost zone, called the epipelagic zone, supports around 90 percent of marine life.

- **The epipelagic zone** is the only ocean zone that gets sunlight. Apart from plants, many species of fish, reptiles and mammals dwell here.

- **The twilight zone** is just below the epipelagic zone. Very little sunlight reaches this zone, making it impossible for plants to survive here. However, deep sea fish are found in this zone.

- **Some animals** living in the twilight zone are bioluminescent. Special organs, called photophores, in the bodies of these animals give off a greenish light.

- **The midnight zone** is the lowest zone and is completely dark and extremely cold. Very few creatures live in this zone and most of them do not have eyes.

- **Oceans** are advanced ecosystems. Tiny plants and animals, called plankton, float on the surface and form the base of the oceanic food chain.

- **Many land creatures** depend on oceans for survival. These include seabirds, and animals such as polar bears. They feed on fish that swim close to the surface.

▼ *Oceans are home to nearly 300,000 different living species, ranging from huge whales to tiny fish.*

Fish facts

▲ *Manta rays belong to the cartilaginous group of fish. Inside a manta ray's mouth are five pairs of gill arches, which filter food from the water. The food particles get trapped in a spongy material between the gill arches, while the water passes out through the ray's gill slits.*

- **Fish are vertebrates**, and like other vertebrates, they have a backbone. They live in water, breathe through their gills and have shiny scales on their bodies.

- **There are more species** of fish than all mammals, reptiles, amphibians and birds put together. Fish are found in varied habitats – from the deepest oceans to the smallest mountain streams.

- **Most fish** live in oceans and just one in five lives in fresh water.

- **Unlike mammals**, fish are cold-blooded. Their body temperature changes with their surroundings.

- **Fish are broadly divided** into two main groups – jawed and jawless. Jawless fish, such as lamprey and hagfish, have a sucker-like mouth with horny teeth. Not many jawless fish exist today.

- **Jawed fish** can be further divided into cartilaginous and bony fish. The skeleton of cartilaginous fish is made up of a strong but flexible tissue called cartilage. Sharks, rays and chimeras are cartilaginous fish.

- **Bony fish** are the most abundant of all fish species. Their skeleton is made up of bones. Most of them have a bladder that helps them swim.

- **Most fish** have a streamlined body that helps them swim better. The sailfish and blue shark are among the fastest swimming fish.

- **Fish feed** on other creatures of the ocean. The smallest of fish feed on microscopic creatures such as zooplankton. Larger fish prey on smaller marine creatures.

- **Fish are very important** to humans as food, since they are a good source of protein. Excessive fishing has endangered some species, while others are already extinct.

Flying fish

- **Flying fish do not actually fly.** Instead, they leap into the air and glide for short distances.

- **The average length** of a flying fish is around 20–30 cm. The California flying fish, found in the Pacific Ocean, is the largest species. It can grow up to a length of 40 cm.

- **The pectoral fins** of flying fish have similar functions to a bird's wings. The two-winged flying fish have very large pectoral fins that they stretch out to soar.

- **Some flying fish** have four 'wings'. In addition to large pectoral fins, these species also have large pelvic fins.

- **When threatened**, flying fish build up speed under the water's surface by thrashing their tails and holding their fins close to the body. The fish then leap into the air and glide for about 20–30 seconds.

- **Flying fish can leap** to a height of about 180 cm and cover a distance of over 150 m. In between glides, the fish returns to the water to gain more speed.

- **They can glide** at double the speed they swim, and are known to accelerate from 36 km/h in water to 72 km/h in air.

- **The ability of flying fish** to take off from the surface of the water and glide for some time help them to escape from sea predators like tuna and mackerel. But once in the air, they become the target of sea birds.

- **Young flying fish** look very different from their parents. The young ones have whiskers on their lower jaw, which disappear when they mature.

- **Flying fish** usually swim in schools. At times, a whole school leaps into the air and glides together.

▲ *Flying fish use their gliding ability effectively to escape predators.*

Herring

- **Herring** are a family of small, silvery marine fish that swim in large schools. They are often found in the temperate, shallow waters of the North Atlantic and the North Pacific.

- **Herring** feed on small fish and plankton. They are, in turn, an important part of the diet of larger creatures such as sharks, seals, whales and seabirds.

- **There are over 360 species** in the herring family, which includes fish such as sardines, anchovies, shad, menhaden and sprats.

- **Sardines** get their name from an island in the Mediterranean, called Sardinia. The fish was once abundant near the coast of this island.

- **The name sardine** refers to various small fish canned with oil or sauce. In the United States, it is another name for herring. However, the true sardine is the young of the pilchard, found off the Mediterranean and Atlantic coasts.

- **The body of herring** is streamlined, making them excellent swimmers. Most herring, sardines and anchovies are less than 90 cm in length.

- **The Atlantic herring** is the best-known variety. The term 'herring' is often applied to this particular variety. The Atlantic herring is believed to be the most abundant species of fish in the world.

> ...FASCINATING FACT...
> The term 'red herring' in detective novels is derived from the smoked and salted processed version of the fish, which takes on reddish hues. Since it gives off a very strong smell, it used to be drawn across hunting trails to confuse dogs. 'Red herring' refers to something that distracts.

- **Atlantic herring** are bluish green in colour, with a silvery underside. The Pacific herring is quite similar to the Atlantic herring.

- **The wolf herring** is the largest of the herring family. It is a fierce hunter and can grow to a length of 3 m.

- **Herring are processed** and sold in several forms. They can be smoked, dried, salted or pickled. Processed herring are sold as kippers, bloaters and red herring.

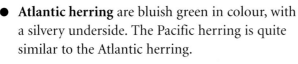

▶ *It is believed that herring swim in huge schools to increase their chances of survival.*

Tuna and mackerel

- **Tuna and mackerel** belong to the *Scombridae* family. Both of them are fast swimmers. Their torpedo-shaped bodies coupled with crescent tails give these fish enough power to thrust through the water at great speeds.

- **Mackerel** have a sleek and shiny body with a large mouth. The head does not have any scales.

▼ *Unlike other ocean fish, tuna have pink flesh. This is because their blood can carry more oxygen. A mackerel's back shows a greeny-blue sheen, while its underside is pale, allowing it to camouflage itself and surprise its prey.*

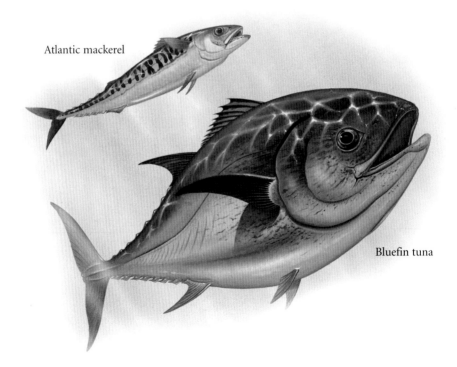

Atlantic mackerel

Bluefin tuna

- **Huge schools of mackerel** can usually be found in cool waters, off the coasts of the northeast United States, Canada, Great Britain and Norway.

- **Mackerel** remain close to the water surface and eat small crabs and fish.

- **The Atlantic mackerel** is the most common variety. It is blue and silver in colour and can grow up to half a metre long. Another equally well-known variety is the chub mackerel, found in the Pacific Ocean.

- **Tuna are found** in most parts of the world. They have a rounded structure and are sleeker than mackerel.

- **Tuna** require a lot of oxygen. These fish swim with their mouth open, shooting jets of water over their gills. The oxygen is extracted from this water. Because of this system of breathing, tuna can never remain still.

- **Unlike most fish**, tuna are not cold-blooded. They are able to maintain a body temperature that is a few degrees warmer than the surrounding water.

- **Tuna** swim in schools and can travel long distances. They come to coastal areas to lay eggs. The eggs usually hatch within 24 hours.

- **Bluefin tuna** are large marine fish. Adults weigh over 680 kg and can swim at a speed of about 90 km/h.

> ...FASCINATING FACT...
> Tuna was sold as a canned product for the first time in 1914. Most consumers at the time thought that the meat tasted like chicken. Hence, the company that marketed canned tuna named their product 'Chicken of the Sea'.

Swordfish

- **Swordfish** are found in tropical and temperate waters. They are mostly dark in colour, but have a lighter coloured belly.

- **Swordfish** get their name from their upper jaw, which extends to form a long sword-like snout with a sharp point. This jaw does not have teeth.

- **The snout** is used for both defence and attack. It is believed that swordfish dash into schools of fish to injure or spear prey with the snout.

- **Like marlin and sailfish**, swordfish are good swimmers. They can swim very long distances in pursuit of prey.

- **Swordfish** have a crescent-shaped tail that is characteristic of fast swimmers belonging to the same family. However, unlike marlin, swordfish do not have pelvic fins.

- **Swordfish swim** near the surface of the water. Some species have been known to swim in schools, but most prefer to be alone.

- **Swordfish feed** on mackerel, herring and other small fish that swim in schools. Sometimes they dive deep into the ocean in search of sardine.

- **Swordfish** can grow over 4 m in length. Their 'sword' accounts for almost one-third of their length. The jaws of a young swordfish are equal in length. The upper jaw grows longer with age.

▼ *Swordfish prefer to swim in water where ocean currents meet.*

- **When attacked**, swordfish can become very violent. It is believed that they can punch holes into small wooden boats. When they are wounded, they thrash about and can cause serious injury.

- **Swordfish** is a popular seafood. The swordfish population has decreased significantly because of overfishing.

Barracuda

- **Barracuda** are powerful predators. In some coastal regions, they are more feared than sharks.

- **Barracuda** are fierce-looking with an elongated head and a long, slender body. Their length varies from 40 cm to almost 2 m.

- **These powerful swimmers** are found in the tropical waters of the Pacific, Atlantic and Indian oceans.

- **The mouth of the barracuda** contains a number of fang-like teeth. These predators have a forked tail, and their dorsal fins are widely separated.

- **The great barracuda**, found in the Pacific and Atlantic oceans, grows to a length of 1.8 m and can be as heavy as 41 kg. Also called the 'tiger of the sea', this aggressive predator is known to attack divers and swimmers.

- **The diet of barracuda** includes sardine, anchovies and squid.

- **Smaller barracuda**, especially those found in the Pacific Ocean, swim and hunt in schools. The larger ones lead a solitary life and hunt alone.

- **Barracuda** are often compared with sharks because of their aggressive nature. But unlike sharks, barracuda do not attack their prey repeatedly.

> **...FASCINATING FACT...**
> Smaller barracudas are eaten by humans. The flesh of species, however, is poisonous because they feed on certain algae-eating smaller fish that are also poisonous. The barracuda are themselves immune to this poison.

- **Barracuda** are guided by their sense of sight rather than smell. Divers avoid wearing bright costumes that can attract these aggressive fish.

- **Their strength** and vigour have made barracuda extremely popular with anglers. Barracuda usually succeed in escaping from the fish hook, making the sport of game fishing more challenging.

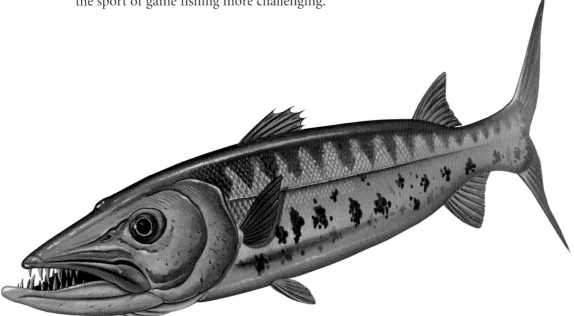

▲ *Barracuda are fearsome predators, which seize, maim and tear up other fish with their fang-like teeth.*

Eels

- **Eels are long**, slender, snake-like fish that live in shallow coastal waters. Most eels live in the sea. However, a few are also found in fresh water.

- **Eels are normally** found among coral reefs and on the ocean floor. There are about 690 species of eels. The most common types include, the conger, moray and gulper eels.

- **Most species** of eel are around 1 m long. However, the conger eel can grow up to 3 m in length.

- **Some moray eels** can grow quite large. A species found in the Pacific Ocean has been known to grow over 3.5 m in length. There are about 100 different species of moray eels.

- **Eels do not have a tail fin**. Their dorsal fin, which runs along the top of the body, makes up for it and provides them with the power to swim.

- **Most eels** do not have scales on their body. Some species, however, have tiny scales. The body of most eels is covered with a slippery layer of mucus.

- **Eels are graceful swimmers** but are not very fast. Some species, like the American eel, can breathe through their skin and can survive for some time out of water.

- **Gulper eels** live at a depth of almost 1000 m. Since light does not reach these parts of the ocean, they have small eyes or none at all. These eels swim with open mouths, ready to gulp down any creature that comes their way.

- **Freshwater eels** travel to the sea to lay eggs. The adults dive deep into the sea to breed and then die.

- **The eggs of freshwater eels** hatch into leaf-shaped larvae that drift about for almost four years. Once they mature, the young eels, called elvers, swim back to the rivers, where they live until it is time for them to breed.

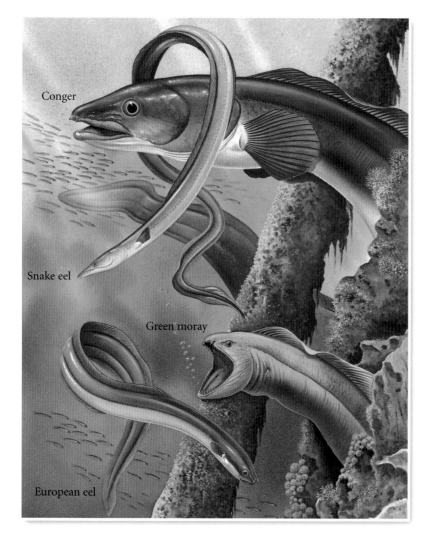

Conger

Snake eel

Green moray

European eel

◀ *There are more than 600 species of eels that are broadly divided into 19 families. Of these, 18 live in the oceans, while one spends part of its life in fresh water.*

Seahorses

- **Seahorses** are tiny creatures that are very different from other fish in appearance. They get their name from their horse-shaped heads.

- **The size** of a seahorse ranges from less than a centimetre to about 13 cm. The common seahorse, found in the northern Atlantic Ocean, is the largest species.

- **Seahorses** have a long, snout-like mouth with tubular jaws and an elongated tail. Their only similarity to fish is the dorsal fin.

- **Seahorses** use their curly tails to attach themselves to coral branches and seaweeds. They swim very slowly by flapping their dorsal fin.

- **Seahorses** live close to seashores across the world. They eat small fish and plankton by swallowing them whole.

- **Instead of scales**, seahorses have a series of large rectangular bony plates. These plates protect them from predators, such as crabs.

- **The pencil-shaped pipefish** belongs to the same family as the seahorse. Like the seahorse, the pipefish too has a long snout with no teeth. It can grow up to a length of about 50 cm.

- **The seahorse family** consists of over 270 species. Others in this family include seadragons, shrimpfish, sea moths and trumpetfish.

- **A female lays** eggs in a pouch on the male's body. The male carries the eggs while they hatch and until the young seahorses are able to swim out through an opening in the pouch.

- **The Chinese** use seahorses to make traditional medicines. Seahorses are also valued as aquarium pets because of their unique shape and colours.

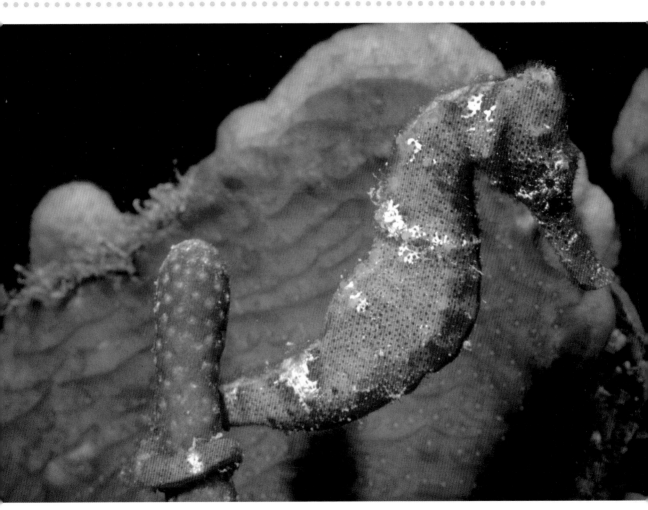

▲ *Seahorses exhibit beautiful, vibrant colours and are usually found swimming among coral reefs.*

Sharks

- **Sharks** belong to the cartilaginous group of fish. There are over 350 species of sharks.

- **Sharks** are found in oceans across the world. Some sharks, like the bull shark, can also survive in fresh water.

- **Most sharks** have torpedo-shaped bodies, making them good swimmers. They also have large tail fins that give them extra power for swimming.

- **A shark's skin** is not covered with smooth scales like bony fish. Instead, its skin is covered with tiny, tooth-like structures called dermal denticles that give the skin a sandpaper-like quality.

- **Sharks** are the primary predators, or hunters, of the ocean. They have special abilities to locate prey. The great white shark, the most feared predator of all, can smell a drop of blood in 100 l of water.

- **The whale shark** is the largest fish. It can grow up to 14 m in length. However, some species, like the spined pygmy shark, are no more than 20 cm long.

- **There are different shapes of shark**. Hammerheads have a T-shaped head, which helps them make sharp turns. Reef-dwelling sharks have a flat body.

- **The diet** of sharks includes seals, squids, fish and other marine creatures. Some sharks, like the whale shark and the basking shark, eat plankton and small fish.

- **Depending upon their diet**, sharks have different kinds of teeth. Some, like the great white and tiger sharks, have sharp pointed teeth that help them tear into their prey.

- **Certain species**, like the reef sharks, have flat plate-like teeth that can crush the hard shells of the animals they eat.

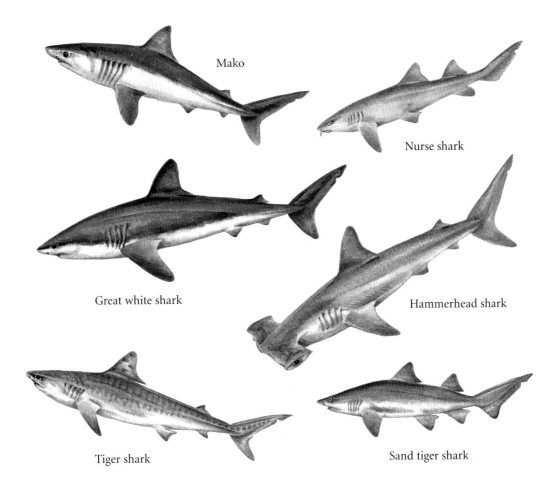

Mako

Nurse shark

Great white shark

Hammerhead shark

Tiger shark

Sand tiger shark

▲ *Six of the most dangerous sharks. All of these sharks have been known to attack people.*

Incredible hunters

▲ *When great white sharks feel threatened, they open their mouths wide to show off sharp teeth.*

- **Sharks** are considered the best hunters in the ocean. These creatures have strong senses that help them hunt and travel great distances.

- **The most powerful weapon** of a shark is its teeth. A shark can have as many as 3000 teeth set in three rows. The fish relies on the first row of teeth to strike the first blow. This first charge often injures or kills the prey.

- **Most sharks** have a very good sense of smell. It is believed that almost one-third of the brain is devoted to detecting smell.

- **Some bottom-dwelling sharks** have thick whisker-like projections on their snouts called nasal barbels. These organs help the shark to feel around for prey.

64

- **Sharks** also have good eyesight. Most of them hunt at night and, like cats, have enhanced night vision. In clear water, sharks can spot their prey from a distance of 15 m.

- **Sharks** do not have external ear flaps. Instead, their ears are inside their head, on either side of the brain case. Each ear leads to a small sensory pore on the shark's head.

- **It is believed** that sharks can hear over a distance of 250 m. They can detect sounds in the frequency of 25–100 Hz.

- **A pair of fluid-filled canals** runs down either side of the shark's body, from its head to its tail. This is the lateral line and helps the fish sense minute vibrations in the water.

- **The lateral line canals** are lined with tiny hair-like projections. These projections are triggered by even the slightest movement, which in turn alert the shark's brain.

- **Most sharks** can detect weak electric currents released by other creatures. They do this with tiny pores located on their snout, which lead to jelly-filled sacs called ampullae of Lorenzini.

...FASCINATING FACT...

Sharks, such as the great white and the blue shark, have a special membrane in their eyes called nictitating membrane. The shark can draw this membrane across its eyes at will. It protects the shark's eyes from being injured by thrashing prey during feeding.

65

Great white shark

- **The great white shark** is the largest predatory shark. It has a pointed snout and a large tail fin. They are commonly found in temperate to warm waters.

- **The great white shark** is actually grey or bluish grey in colour, with a white underbelly. It is also known as 'white pointer' and 'white death'.

- **One of the biggest of all sharks**, the great white, is normally about 4.5 m in length. However, it is believed that some can grow as long as 6 m.

- **Great white sharks** have around 3000 sharp teeth with serrated, or saw-like, edges. The shark's teeth can grow up to 7.5 cm long.

- **The diet** of this shark includes sea lions, seals and sea turtles. Young great whites eat fish, rays and other smaller sharks.

- **Great white sharks** do not chew their food. They use their sharp teeth to rip the prey into small pieces that are then swallowed whole.

- **The shark usually** approaches prey, such as seals, from below. Sometimes, while chasing seals, the shark leaps out of water. This is called breaching.

- **Unlike other sharks**, great whites do not have a gas-filled swim bladder to keep them afloat. Therefore, they have to keep swimming to stay afloat.

- **The great white shark** does not lay eggs like other fish. The eggs remain inside the female's body until they hatch. The shark then gives birth to live young.

> **...FASCINATING FACT...**
> The great white shark is feared because of its reputation as a man-eater. Although the reports of great white attacks are true, the shark has been responsible for only 58 deaths since 1876!

● **A surfer**, when viewed from below, looks very similar to a seal – the favourite food of the great white. Most biologists believe that this is the reason for great white attacks on surfers.

▲ *The massive great white shark has been reported to have attacked boats, even sinking one near Nova Scotia, Canada.*

Hammerhead shark

- **Hammerhead sharks** have a thick, wide hammer-shaped head. Their eyes are located on either side of this T-shaped head.

- **The head contains** tiny receptors that detect the prey. Its unusual shape also helps the shark to take sharp turns.

- **The hammerhead** is common in tropical and temperate waters. It is grey or brown in colour, with an off-white belly. This shark migrates towards warmer waters near the Equator in winter.

- **The first dorsal fin** of the hammerhead, which is located on its back, is large and pointed. Like most sharks, it can be seen cutting through the water surface, as the hammerhead cruises along.

- **The great hammerhead** is the largest in the hammerhead family. It can measure up to 4 m in length. Bonnethead sharks are smaller and have a shovel-like head.

- **Hammerhead sharks** normally feed on fish, smaller sharks, squid and octopuses. Stingrays, however, are their favourite food.

- **The great hammerhead** is an excellent hunter. It uses its highly developed senses of smell and direction to track prey.

- **Large teeth** enable the great hammerhead to bite big chunks off its prey.

- **Other varieties of hammerhead** sharks include the scalloped and the smooth hammerhead. Both types are found in moderately temperate waters.

- **Most hammerheads** are harmless, but the great hammerhead is one of the few dangerous species. It is known to have attacked humans.

◀ *A scalloped hammerhead shark cruises across a coral reef – an underwater structure built by tiny creatures called coral polyps.*

Whale shark

- **Whale sharks** are the largest fish in the world. They are not aggressive and pose no threat to humans.

- **Whale sharks** prefer to live in warm tropical waters and are found in many areas across the world. They are rarely found in temperate waters.

- **The average length** of a whale shark is about 14 m. However, some have been known to grow to over 18 m in length.

- **These gentle giants** are also very heavy. An average adult whale shark weighs about 15 tonnes. Owing to their size, these sharks cannot move fast. They swim by moving their enormous bodies from side to side.

- **Whale sharks** are dark-grey or brown in colour and their underside is off-white. They have white dots and lines on their backs.

- **The mouth** of the whale shark is extremely large and can be as wide as 1.4 m. They have around 300 rows of tiny, hook-like teeth in each jaw.

- **These sharks** move about with their mouths open and suck in vast quantities of water, rich in plankton. Special bristles attached to the gills filter the tiny prey, while the water is thrown out through the gill slits.

- **Whale sharks** have a huge appetite. They feed mainly on plankton, sardines, krill and anchovies.

- **These sharks** also love to eat fish eggs. They are known to wait for hours at breeding grounds to capture freshly laid eggs. They also return to the same mating grounds year after year during the breeding season.

- **Sometimes**, whale sharks can be seen swimming in schools. However, they usually travel alone.

▼ *The whale shark has patterns of light spots and stripes on a dark body. These help the shark to blend into its surroundings.*

Rays

- **Rays are cartilaginous fish**. Unlike bony fish, their skeletons are not made up of bones. Instead they are made of a tough, elastic tissue called cartilage.

- **Sharks and chimaeras**, or ratfish, belong to the same group of fish as rays.

- **Rays are found** in oceans across the world. Most rays live near the seabed. When in danger, they bury themselves in the sand.

▲ *The spotted eagle ray is identified by the distinct spots on its back, which can be white, yellow or green in colour.*

- **These fish** have broad, flat bodies. Their eyes are located on the upper surface of the body, while the mouth and gills are on the lower side.

- **Rays are usually brown** or black in colour, but their underside is lighter. Certain species change their colour to match the surroundings, which makes them hard to spot.

- **Some species** are less than 10 cm in width, while others measure over 6 m across. Manta rays are the biggest of all rays.

- **The pectoral fins** of rays are located just behind their heads. These huge, wing-like fins stretch from both sides of the head to the tail. The ray uses its 'wings' to swim through the water.

- **Rays' tails** vary in size and structure. While most rays have a long tail, some have a short, broad one. Rays use their tail as a rudder while swimming and also to defend themselves.

- **Different species** of rays have different forms of defence. The long, whip-like tail of the stingray has one or more sharp spines that inject poison into prey.

- **Most species** of rays feed on crustaceans, such as crabs, krill and shrimps. The manta ray, however, prefers to eat plankton.

> ····FASCINATING FACT····
> The electric ray, also called the 'torpedo', has a pair of
> large electric organs between its head and pectoral fins.
> These organs can give powerful shocks, measuring up
> to 200 volts. These shocks can stun or even kill prey.

Whales

- **Whales** are among the largest and heaviest animals on the planet. Their size can range from 2–3 m to over 30 m.

- **Being mammals**, whales breathe with their lungs. They do not have gills. The nostrils of whales, called blowholes, are located on top of the head.

- **When underwater**, whales need to hold their breath. They come up to the surface and open their blowholes to breathe. After taking in the required amount of air, these animals dive into the water again. The blowholes remain closed underwater.

- **The spout, or blow** that can be seen rising from the blowhole is not water. It is actually stale air that condenses and vaporizes the moment it is released into the atmosphere. This spout can sometimes reach a height of 10 m.

- **Whales** are divided into two main groups: toothed whales and baleen whales. Together, these groups consist of 81 known species.

- **Toothed whales** have small teeth in their jaws, which are used to kill prey like fish and squid. This group includes dolphins, killer whales, sperm whales, beluga whales and porpoises.

- **Toothed whales** emit sound waves that are bounced off an object, revealing its size, shape and location. This is known as echolocation.

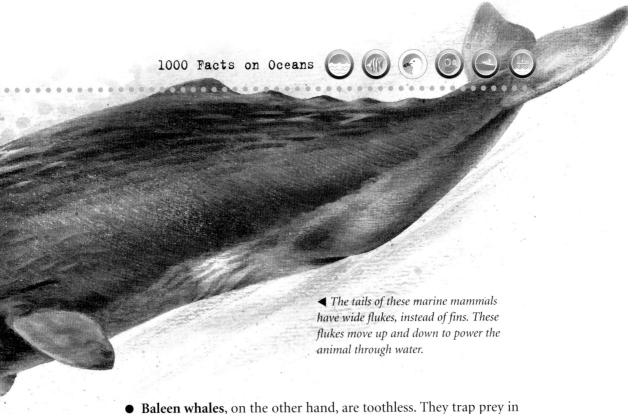

◀ *The tails of these marine mammals have wide flukes, instead of fins. These flukes move up and down to power the animal through water.*

- **Baleen whales**, on the other hand, are toothless. They trap prey in sieve-like structures hanging from their upper jaws.
- **Baleen whales** are also known as great whales. This group includes grey, humpback, right and the mighty blue whale.

...FASCINATING FACT...
Toothed whales use the echolocation technique to distinguish between prey and non-prey objects.

75

Baleen and blubber

- **Baleen whales** have a huge mouth that contains rows of baleen plates. These plates have fringed edges like a comb that filter plankton from the water.

- **Whales** of this group swim with their mouths open and take in thousands of litres of water containing krill and other small marine creatures. These creatures get trapped in the fringed edges of the baleen. The whale licks the food off the baleen and swallows it.

▲ *Humpback whales, like all baleen whales, are filter feeders.*

- **Baleen**, also called whalebone, was once valued for its plastic-like attributes. Great whales were widely hunted for their baleen. However, with the wide availability of good-quality plastic, the demand for baleen has diminished.

- **Heat loss is greater** in water than it is on land at the same temperature. Whales have a thick layer of fat, called blubber, between the skin and the flesh that preserves body heat.

- **Blubber also helps** to keep the animals afloat and is a source of stored energy. Until recently, it was extensively used in the manufacture of cosmetics and ointments.

- **Toothed whales** have smaller mouths than great whales. However, unlike meat-eating animals of the land, the teeth of these whales are uniform in size and shape.

- **Most whales swim** and feed in groups called pods. Many whales are known to migrate long distances between their feeding places and breeding grounds.

- **Whales** sometimes pop their head above the surface and float motionless. This is known as 'logging'.

- **Some whales**, like humpback whales, are very acrobatic and can leap out of the water. This is known as 'breaching'. They also indulge in 'lob-tailing' – sticking out their tail and then splashing it in the water.

- **Some whales** also lift their head vertically out of the water before slipping back below. This is known as 'spyhopping'. It is believed that they do this to obtain a view above the surface.

Blue whale

- **Blue whales** are the largest creatures to have ever lived on this planet. They are even larger than the mighty dinosaurs that lived millions of years ago.

- **Their average length** is 25 m but some can grow to more than 30 m. *Brachiosaurus*, the largest dinosaur, was only 20–25 m long.

- **These whales** are blue-grey in colour with light patches on the back. Sometimes, the underside of this animal can be yellowish in colour. This is caused by a kind of algae and has given the blue whale the nickname 'sulphurbottom'.

- **The body** is streamlined with a large tail fin. The dorsal fin is small, while the tail is thick and large. Blue whales have splashguards in front of their two blowholes.

- **Blue whales** are migratory animals. They live near the tropics during winter and migrate towards icy waters in summer.

- **The diet** of a blue whale consists of small fish, plankton and krill in enormous quantities. They can eat over 4 tons of krill every day.

- **These whales** have been known to gather in groups of 60 or more. However, they are largely solitary animals.

- **The spout** of a blue whale is vertical and can be 10–12 m high.

- **Blue whales** are relatively slow swimmers. However, when threatened, these animals can swim at a speed of over 30 km/h.

- **Merciless hunting** over several decades has caused the blue whale population to decline drastically. It is currently an endangered species, and only 5000 are thought to exist worldwide.

▼ *Blue whales have 300–400 pairs of baleen plates that they use to strain food from the water. The calves feed on their mother's rich milk until they are around eight months old.*

Killer whale

- **Killer whales,** also known as orcas, are the largest dolphins. Despite their name, killer whales have more in common with dolphins than with great whales. Hence they are considered a part of the dolphin family.

- **They have a black body** with white patches on their underside and behind each eye.

- **These animals** are found in oceans across the world, but prefer to live in colder temperate waters. They do not migrate in summer like great whales but can swim for long distances.

- **Killer whales** prefer to live close to the coast. Their average length is 8–10 m. They have sharp, hooked teeth, which they use to rip their prey apart.

- *Dephinus orca* was the earliest scientific name for the killer whale. It meant 'demon dolphin'.

- **It is believed** that the name 'killer whale' might itself have been derived from the name 'whale killer'. This name was given to these animals by 18th century whalers who saw them feeding on other whales and dolphins.

- **The diet of orcas** is varied. However, they largely prey on fish, squid, sharks and warm-blooded animals such as seals, seabirds and larger whales, including blue whales.

- **Orcas are known** as the 'wolves of the sea'. Like wolves, they hunt in groups and hence are able to tackle prey of all shapes and sizes.

- **The pods of killer whales** are divided into resident and transient pods. Resident pods can consist of 5–50 members who communicate frequently using whistles and high-pitched screams.

- **Transient pods** are smaller, with a maximum of seven members who feed mainly on marine mammals. Members of transient pods do not communicate frequently with each other.

▲ Killer whales live in groups called pods. The older females are in charge. Their offspring may stay together for 10 to 20 years.

Humpback whale

- **Humpback whales** are large baleen whales. They are one of the most active whales and can often be seen leaping out of the water.

- **These whales** are found in most parts of the world. During summer they migrate to the icy waters in the north and south. In winter, they breed in warm, tropical waters.

- **They have a round**, flat head that has fleshy bumps called tubercles. The body is black or grey, with mottled white patches. The underside is off-white.

- **The humpback** grows up to 15 m in length. At almost 5 m, its flippers are the longest among whales. The animal is named after a hump on which the whale's dorsal fin is located. This is most pronounced when the whale dives.

- **The tail fin** measures nearly 5.5 m across and has black and white patterns. Since no two humpback whales have the same pattern on their tails, scientists use it to identify and monitor them.

- **They feed** on shrimps, krill and small fish. Humpbacks have various methods of feeding. These include lunge-feeding, tail-flicking and bubble-netting.

- **In lunge-feeding**, the humpback opens its mouth wide and swims through a group of prey, often coming to the surface with food in its mouth.

- **When tail-flicking**, the whale lies with its belly just below the surface. It uses its tail to flick the prey into the air and down its mouth.

- **Bubble-netting** is the most spectacular of all feeding habits and the most commonly used by the humpback. The whale slaps its flippers around a school of fish, creating a wall of bubbles. This action forces the fish to move to the surface in large groups, making them easy prey.

● **Male humpbacks** are known for their unusual and eerie songs. The sounds vary from high-pitched squeaks to deep wails and can last for half an hour or more. These songs are usually heard during the breeding season.

▲ *Humpbacks have lots of lumps and bumps on their heads called tubercles. Hard-shelled sea creatures called barnacles also live there.*

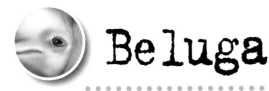

Beluga

- **Beluga whales** are fascinating creatures. Their playful nature, along with their unusual colour, makes them popular attractions in aquariums.

- **Related to dolphins**, the adult beluga whale is milky white in colour. Its name is derived from the Russian word *belukha*, meaning white.

- **The colour** of the whale matches its surroundings. This whale lives close to icebergs in the Arctic Ocean. Young belugas, however, are grey in colour.

- **They have narrower** necks compared with other whales. Unlike most other baleen and toothed whales, belugas can also nod and shake their heads from side to side.

- *Delphinapterus leucas*, the scientific name of the beluga, means 'white dolphin without wings', referring to the absence of a dorsal fin in this species.

- **The beluga's diet** consists of crab, squid, shrimp and fish. They love salmon and often swim into the mouths of rivers to feed on them. They use their teeth to grab prey rather than to chew.

- **Belugas** are very social and tend to travel in groups consisting of 5–20 members. These groups are usually led by a single male. During migrations, the groups can exceed 10,000 members.

- **These whales** emit various sounds, from whistles to chirps and squeaks. They are the most vocal whales, earning them the nickname of sea canaries.

- **Belugas** are hunted by killer whales. The young are often killed by polar bears. It is not uncommon to find adult belugas bearing scars from polar bear attacks.

...FASCINATING FACT...
Belugas do not have a dorsal fin, which
makes swimming under ice much easier.

▼ *Belugas have a thick, stout body, a
small beak and a prominent forehead,
which is called a 'melon'.*

Dolphins

- **Dolphins** are close relatives of whales and form a large part of the toothed whales group. They have a beak-shaped snout and are extremely active and playful.

- **They are found** in all oceans, and are powerful swimmers. The shape of their body and their big flippers help in rapid movement. Dolphins are often spotted riding on waves, probably to conserve energy.

- **Dolphins** are good at diving deep into the ocean and also leaping into the air. Many of them can leap as high as 7 m. They can even turn somersaults before landing into the water with a splash.

- **Like baleen whales**, dolphins have blowholes on top of their head. They surface every two minutes to breathe, before diving under again.

- **Dolphins** use echolocation to hunt and navigate through cloudy waters. They emit a series of high-pitched sound pulses, which bounce off prey or obstacles, enabling dolphins to locate them.

- **These animals** hunt in groups. They chase their prey, surround it, and catch it with their powerful jaws. Dolphins have numerous conical teeth.

- **The smallest dolphin** is the tucuxi dolphin, which is hardly 1 m long. Bottlenose dolphins can reach a length of over 3.5 m, while common dolphins are about 2.5 m long.

> ... FASCINATING FACT ...
> Some scientists believe that dolphins have a language of their own, heard by humans in the form of whistling sounds. Some even believe that they are able to understand sign language.

● **The killer whale** is the largest member of the dolphin family. It can reach a length of almost 10 m. Like others in the family, the killer whale is very intelligent and can be trained to do tricks.

● **The playful nature** of dolphins has made them extremely popular, especially with children. They are common sights in sea life centres.

● **Dolphins used** to be hunted for their meat and oil. Until recently, thousands used to die every year by getting caught in fishing nets.

▲ *Bottlenose dolphins usually swim at speeds of 5–11 km/h, but sometimes they can exceed 32 km/h.*

Porpoises

- **Porpoises** are small, toothed whales. They are close relatives of dolphins, and are often mistaken for them.

- **They are usually smaller than dolphins**, and not as sleek and streamlined. Porpoises rarely grow to more than 2.2 m. They are usually grey, blue or black in colour.

▼ *While on the move, the harbour porpoise surfaces six to eight times within one minute. Normally, they can stay under water for about 5 minutes before surfacing again.*

- **The dorsal fin** of a porpoise is triangular, whereas the dolphin's is curved. Porpoises do not have a beak.

- **There are several varieties** of porpoises, including Dall's and the spectacled porpoise. The harbour porpoise, also called the common porpoise, is the best known.

- **Harbour porpoises** are found in cold, northern waters and are known to frequent bays and estuaries. They have a small body and dorsal fin.

- **There are two varieties** of Dall's porpoises – the *dalli* type and the *truei* type. Both are found in the northern Pacific Ocean.

- **Dall's porpoises** are known for the splash they make in the water with their tails. This is referred to as the 'rooster-tail splash', and has earned this species the other name of 'spray porpoise'.

- **Another well-known species** is the spectacled porpoise, found in the South Atlantic. The upper part of its body is bluish black, while the lower half is white.

- **Spectacled porpoises** have black patches around their eyes, which are surrounded by a white line. These resemble spectacles.

- **Other varieties of porpoise** include Burmeister's porpoises, which is commonly found off the coasts of South America. It is named after the German biologist Burmeister, who gave this species the scientific name *spinipinnis,* meaning spiny fin. This was due to the blunt, thorn-like structures, called tubercles, along the edges of the porpoise's fins.

89

Seals

- **Seals** are marine mammals, which belong to the same group as walruses and sea lions. Together these animals are called pinnipeds, which means 'fin-footed'. All of them have limbs that look like fins.

- **There are two families of seals**: true seals and eared seals. Unlike eared seals, true seals do not have external ear flaps.

- **There are 19 species of true seals,** making them the largest group of pinnipeds. Eared seals consist of sea lions and fur seals.

- **The limbs of seals** are modified into powerful flippers that help in swimming. Their strong, torpedo-shaped body, coupled with the ability to store oxygen, make them great swimmers.

- **Eared seals** have long rear flippers that are more mobile than those of true seals. Their front flippers are also large and more powerful. Eared seals mainly use their front flippers to paddle through water.

- **Seals** spend most of their lives in water, but they have to come ashore to breed and nurse their young. Some live at sea for several months at a time, while others return to the shore every day.

- **Most species** live in cold regions. They have a thick coat of fur that keeps them warm. They also have a layer of fat, called 'blubber', under their skin, which provides warmth and a storehouse of energy when food is scarce.

- **Seals** range in size from 1–4 m. Galapagos fur seals and ringed seals are the smallest species. The largest is the male southern elephant seal, which can grow to 5 m in length.

- **The diet** of seals consists mainly of fish, squid, crabs and shellfish. Leopard seals are among the most aggressive hunters. They kill other seals and penguins for food. They are also known to have injured divers.

- **Killer whales**, sharks and polar bears are the natural predators of seals. They are endangered because of excessive hunting by man for their meat, fat and fur. The Caribbean monk seal is now extinct due to excessive hunting.

▼ *Seals are clumsy on land. They slide along the shore with difficulty. However, the large flippers of eared seals are better adapted for moving on land.*

Sea lions

- **Sea lions** are eared seals. Unlike true seals, they have external ear flaps and their flippers are quite big.

- **These extremely vocal animals** make a roaring noise, which gives them their name. They are brownish in colour, with the males being darker than the females.

- **Sea lions** use their flippers to swim and paddle in water as well as walk on land. They can use their flippers as legs.

- **Being highly social creatures**, sea lions swim in large groups.

- **Steller's sea lion** is the largest type of sea lion. The males can grow up to 3 m in length. They are found in the northern waters of the Pacific Ocean, and are very common off Alaska.

- **The diet** of a sea lion includes mainly fish, crab, squid, octopus and clams. Steller's sea lion also feed on seals and small otters.

- **Steller's sea lion** and California sea lion are the best-known species. The former are tamed very easily and are popular attractions in water parks.

- **California sea lions** are found along the rocky western coast of North America. They are also found on the Galapagos Islands. The males are over 2 m in length and the females are smaller.

- **Killer whales** are the biggest enemies of sea lions. Sharks are also known to hunt California sea lions.

- **A large number** of sea lions die as a result of getting caught in fishing nets. There are now laws restricting the hunting of sea lions. Steller's sea lion has been declared as endangered.

▼ *Sea lions nurse their pups for about a year. Duing this period they leave their pups to go hunting in the sea and return after five days to continue nursing.*

Sea cows

- **Manatees and dugongs** are both types of sea cow. They are large, thick-bodied mammals. Apart from whales and dolphins, sea cows are the only other mammals that live completely in water.

▲ *A diver tagging a manatee. Florida manatees usually swim at a speed of 3–10 km/h or less. However, they can manage speeds of about 24 km/h for short bursts.*

- **Dugongs** are found in the tropical waters of the Indian and Pacific oceans, while manatees are found off the Caribbean Islands, the southeast United States and West Africa.

- **Sea cows** graze on seagrasses and other aquatic plants, hence the name 'sea cow'. There are only four living species in this group, of which three belong to the manatee family.

- **Sea cows** are also called sirenians, after the Sirens, or mermaids, of Greek mythology. It is believed that sailors probably mistook sea cows for creatures that were half human and half fish, thus giving rise to the mermaid legends.

- **Steller's sea cow**, one of the largest species, is now extinct. It was killed for its meat and skin. Since this slow-moving mammal could not defend itself the population was completely wiped out.

- **Steller's sea cow** was first discovered in the Arctic waters in 1741 by the crew of the famous Russian explorer, Captain Vitus Bering.

- **Manatees have a long**, rounded body that tapers towards the tail. Their average length is 3.5 m. They have a short, square snout, and are mostly grey in colour.

- **Dugongs and manatees** are closely related to elephants. Dugongs are very similar to manatees in both looks and habits, although some are slightly smaller.

- **Both manatees and dugongs** are slow swimmers and use their forelimbs and tails to move in the water. They do not have hind limbs.

- **Unlike the dugong**, the manatee's forelimbs are set very close to its head. The tail of the dugong is forked and pointed like a whale's, while the manatee has a round, flat, paddle-like tail.

Gulls

▶ *Larger species of gulls, such as this common gull, attain their full plumage within four years, while the smaller ones take only two years.*

- **A large number** of birds live around the oceans. Of these, gulls, or seagulls, are the most common. These birds are migratory, and there are about 43 species around the world.

- **Gulls** range in length from 28 cm to 80 cm. Most species have white and grey plumage or feathers. Some have black markings on the back, wings and head.

96

- **These birds** have a sharp, hooked bill, which helps them kill small birds and similar prey. They also have webbed feet to paddle on water surfaces. Gulls cannot dive underwater.

- **Gulls** use the wind to stay aloft without flapping their wings.

- **The colour** of the plumage changes throughout the gull's life. Some even have a different winter and summer plumage.

- **Black-headed gulls** have dark heads and red-coloured bills in summer. In winter, however, the heads of these species turn white with a dark grey spot. It is believed that this gives the bird better camouflage in the snow.

- **Many gulls** venture inland and hunt among garbage for food. They are also great scavengers and feed on dead animal matter along seashores.

- **Gulls** are able to fish in shallow waters and often prey on the eggs of other seabirds. Some of them even feed on eggs laid by their own species.

- **Gulls** make simple grass-lined nests, mostly on flat ground in isolated areas of beaches. Some nest on ledges in cliffs.

- **Commonly found** species include herring, common, black-headed and ring-billed gulls. The great black-backed gull is the largest of all.

...FASCINATING FACT...
Gulls might be popularly called seagulls but very few species actually venture into the open seas. Most prefer to keep to the shore, while some come to the coast only during the breeding season.

Albatrosses

▶ *Albatrosses are also known as goonie or gooney birds. Once airborne, these graceful creatures can glide for hours without flapping their wings.*

- **The albatross** is the largest seabird, weighing about 12 kg. It is commonly found in oceans of the southern hemisphere, but some species also dwell in the North Pacific.

- **Most albatrosses** are white or pale grey in colour, with black wing tips. Some albatrosses have shades of brown.

- **The wandering albatross** has the largest wingspan of all birds, at about 3.7 m. It can grow up to 1.4 m in length, with females being smaller than males.

- **Albatrosses** have a sharp bill with a hooked upper jaw. They also have tubular nostrils and webbed feet. Their long, narrow wings make them powerful gliders.

- **These birds** are so heavy that they have to leap from cliffs to launch into flight.

- **Albatrosses** prey on squid, cuttlefish and small marine creatures. Unlike gulls, these large birds can drink seawater.

- **Of all seabirds** albatrosses spend the most time at sea. They even sleep while floating on the surface of the ocean. They come ashore only during the breeding season.

- **Albatrosses** nest in colonies on remote islands. Most of them have complex mating dances and may even change colour during courtship.

- **These birds** can travel thousands of kilometres. Adult albatrosses often go out into the sea in search of food for their young. Since the distances are great, the parents swallow the prey and regurgitate the food into the chick's mouth when they arrive back at the nest.

- **There is a superstition** among sailors that killing an albatross brings bad luck. This belief forms the theme of Samuel Taylor Coleridge's famous poem *The Rime of the Ancient Mariner.*

Pelicans

- **Pelicans** can be easily identified by their long bill and massive throat pouch. They are strong swimmers and the largest diving birds.

- **They are big birds**, with a long neck and short legs. Adult pelicans grow up to 1.8 m in length and weigh 4–7 kg. Males are larger than females. Their wing span can measure up to 3 m.

- **There are seven species** of pelicans. All are found in warmer climates. Most pelicans can also live near bodies of fresh water. The brown pelican, however, is excusively a seabird.

- **Most pelicans** are white, except for brown and Peruvian pelicans, which are dark in colour. American white pelicans have black wing tips.

- **Pelicans** breed in colonies. Nearly 40,000 birds come together on isolated shores or islands to breed.

- **In some species**, the colour of the bill and pouch changes during the mating season. The front part of the pouch turns a bright salmon pink, while the base becomes deep yellow. Parts of the bill change to bright blue and a black strip can be seen from the base to the tip.

- **The female pelican** builds a nest by digging a hole in the ground using her bill and feet. She then lines the hole with grass, leaves and feathers. Three days later, she lays about three eggs in her new nest.

- **While fishing**, this bird uses its pouch as a net to catch the prey. Once the prey is caught, the pelican draws the pouch close to its chest to empty the water out and swallow the prey. Food is also carried in the pouch and later retrieved to feed the chicks.

- **Different species** have different hunting techniques. Brown and Peruvian pelicans dive headlong into the water to catch fish.

- **Most other pelicans** swim and then pounce on their prey. Some fish in groups and drive the fish towards shallow waters where it is easier to capture them. Pelicans feed on small fish and crustaceans.

▼ *The American white pelican does not dive for its food but prefers to fish in large groups.*

Penguins

▲ *A penguin and chicks. These social birds like to live in large groups.*

- **Penguins** are big sea birds that cannot fly. There are about 17 species of penguins, most of which live in the Antarctic region.

- **Some species** are found as far north as the Galapagos Islands. Smaller penguin species are found in warmer waters.

- **Larger penguins** are better at retaining heat, so they can live closer to the South Pole. The emperor penguin is the tallest at 1.2 m, while the smallest is the fairy penguin, or the little blue penguin, which is less then 40 cm in height.

- **Penguins** have a thick layer of fat that protects them from the freezing temperatures of the region. Their coats are waterproof.

- **These flightless birds** have black heads and wings, and a white underside. They have sharp bills and a short tail.

- **Penguins** do not use their wings for flying. Instead the wings act like flippers that help them swim. These birds are good divers and swimmers and can move in water at great speeds in search of small fish and krill.

- **On land**, penguins waddle about clumsily. They are often seen sliding down slopes on their bellies.

- **Adélie penguins** are known to waddle over 300 km every year to reach their breeding grounds. These birds depend on the Sun to navigate across the ice. Once the sun sets they are at risk of losing their way.

- **Rockhopper penguins** have a tuft of yellow feathers on their head. They are called rockhoppers because they jump around from rock to rock.

- **Penguins** have been hunted extensively by humans for their fat and skin. Their natural enemies are sharks, whales and leopard seals.

Sea turtles

- **There are only seven species** of marine turtles. They are found in tropical and sub-tropical waters around the world.

- **The leatherback turtle** is the largest sea turtle. The other species are loggerhead, hawksbill, olive ridley, Kemp's ridley, flatback and green sea turtles.

- **A hard shell** covers and protects the sea turtle's body. Compared to the freshwater turtle, the sea turtle has a flatter, less domed shell, which helps it to swim faster.

- **The front limbs** of the sea turtle are larger than the back limbs. These flipper-like limbs help the turtle to 'fly' through the water, although moving on land is quite awkward.

Loggerhead turtle

Hawksbill turtle

Green turtle

Leatherback turtle

▲ *Turtles only come ashore to lay their eggs. Although they are born on land, turtles head for the sea the minute they hatch.*

- **The shell** of the leatherback sea turtle is made of a thick, rubbery substance that is strengthened by small bones. These turtles are named after this unusual shell.

- **Sea snakes and sea turtles** are the only reptiles that spend most of their lives in the ocean. The females swim ashore for a few hours each year to lay eggs.

- **Sea turtles** prefer to lay their eggs at night. The female digs a pit in the sand with her flippers. She then lays about 50–150 eggs, and covers the nest with sand.

- **Once the eggs hatch** the young turtles struggle out of their sandpit and make their way to the sea. On the way, many babies fall prey to seabirds, crabs, otters and other predators.

- **The diet of sea turtles** differs from species to species. Leatherbacks prefer jellyfish, while olive ridleys and loggerheads eat hard-shelled creatures such as crabs. Sponges are a favourite of hawksbills.

- **Most turtle species** are under threat because they are hunted for their eggs, meat and shells. The trade in turtles has been declared illegal in most countries, but people continue to kill them.

> ...FASCINATING FACT...
> It is believed that sea turtles have been on our planet for
> over 100 million years. They have survived, while other
> prehistoric animals, such as dinosaurs, have become extinct.

Sea snakes

- **Sea snakes** are mainly found in the warm waters of the Indian and Pacific oceans. They can be ten times more venomous than most land snakes.

- **Sea snakes feed on small fish**, eels and fish eggs. They use their venom to kill their prey, and then swallow it whole.

▼ *Sea snakes use venom (poison) to stun prey. The venom of sea snakes is more powerful than that of any land snake.*

Banded sea snake

Yellow-bellied sea snake

- **The scales** on a sea snake are small. This reduces friction, and helps the animal to swim faster. The sea snake also has a flat, paddle-like tail that aids in swimming.

- **Being reptiles**, sea snakes do not have gills. They have to come up to the surface of the water to breathe. However, they are able to absorb some oxygen from the water that they swallow. This helps them stay underwater for longer periods.

- **The sea snake** has a special gland under its tongue that gets rid of excess salt from sea water. It also has highly developed nostril valves that can be closed while diving into the depths of the ocean.

- **There are two kinds of sea snakes**. Aquatic sea snakes never leave the water, not even to breed, while amphibious sea snakes, or sea kraits, slither on to land to lay their eggs.

- **Aquatic sea snakes,** or 'true' sea snakes, are viviparous. This means that the female does not lay eggs, but gives birth to live young.

- **The yellow-bellied sea snake** is the most easily recognized 'true' sea snake. It is named after its bright yellow belly. Although this snake is extremely poisonous, it attacks only when disturbed.

- **This sea snake** can also swim backwards and is the fastest swimmer amongst sea snakes, reaching a speed of 3.6 km/h. It is also capable of staying underwater for three hours before coming up to the surface to breathe.

- **Sea kraits** have coloured bands on their body. Unlike 'true' sea snakes, sea kraits have wide scales on their bellies that help them to move on land.

The first boats

- **Based on drawings and models** found in Egypt, there is evidence that boats date back as far as 6000BC. In fact, recent studies suggest that boats were common in Asia and Africa even before that.

- **Wood** was the most popular material used to build boats in ancient times. In some ancient civilizations, such as Mesopotamia, boats were made of animal skin stretched over bones.

- **Later coracles**, or round boats covered with animal skin, were developed. These boats had wicker frames and were used mainly for fishing.

- **Kayaks** were another type of skin boat. They were used by the Inuit in Greenland for whaling. Kayaks are used even today, but mostly for recreation.

- **Dugouts** soon replaced skin boats. At first, dugouts were merely hollowed-out tree trunks. Later these hollows were made watertight by either inserting a separate piece of wood, called a transom, on both ends, or by sealing the ends with clay.

- **The Egyptians** built rafts by tying papyrus reeds together. These lightweight boats were used for fishing and for transporting light goods on the Nile. Later, the need to transport heavier cargo led the Egyptians to build stronger wooden boats.

> ...FASCINATING FACT...
> The Chinese made strong ships, known as 'junks'. These shipshad a number of large sails usually made of linen, and were steeredby rudders, or movable blades on the stern. The junks were largely used to transport cargo. However, in several parts of China, they also served as houses and schools.

- **Egyptian rafts** were made from planks of wood tied together. Unfortunately they were not very sturdy and were used only for trips along rivers and coasts.

- **Gradually sails** were developed, which could harness wind energy and move boats at a greater speed. Sails were first developed by the Egyptians, in 3500BC. They equipped their reed boats with square sails.

- **The Phoenicians** developed the sail further. They were mainly traders and needed to travel long distances. During the period 1500–1000BC, they developed excellent sail boats.

- **Shipbuilding** received a boost during the age of exploration, from AD1000 to 1500. The Vikings and the Portuguese and Spanish sailors went on long voyages, which required fast, sturdy and dependable ships.

▶ *The word 'junk' is said to have come from the Chinese word* jung, *meaning 'floating house'.*

109

Ancient cargo ships

- **In ancient Mesopotamia**, which is in modern-day Iraq, the earliest boats were of three types. These were wooden boats with triangular sails, tub-shaped boats called *Guffa*, which were made from reeds and animal skins, and rafts made of timber and inflated animal skins, called *kalakku*.

- **The *kalakku*** did not have sails. Instead, it relied on currents to float downstream. Once the boat reached its destination, the cargo was offloaded and the boat, dismantled. It was then transported upstream on donkeys.

- **Massive clay pots** were used as floats. Animal skins were stretched across the inner and outer surfaces of the pots to keep them waterproof.

- **Reeds were used** by ancient Egyptians to make rafts that could carry goods across the Nile. These boats did not last long but were easy to build.

- **The earliest wooden boats** were simple structures. They were either pieces of log tied together or hollowed-out tree trunks. They could only carry a small amount of cargo.

- **With the need to transport** more cargo, the simple wooden boats were modified. Sails were first developed in Egypt in about 3500BC and were used in reed boats built to transport large stones.

- **The invention of the sail** revolutionized shipbuilding as it resulted in the ability to move large boat hulls. This allowed the transportation of large quantities of cargo at one time.

- **The Phoenicians** were the most skilled shipbuilders of ancient times. They made huge merchant vessels, with strong wooden hulls, capable of carrying large amounts of cargo.

▶ *Ancient Phoenician trading ships had broad beams, a sail and two stern oars. A large clay amphora containing drinking water was attached to the stem posts of these ships.*

- **While most ancient boats** were small and used to transport cargo down rivers, ocean-going vessels were being made in Asia.

- **People of the Indus Valley civilization** are believed to have used ships to trade with other civilizations such as Mesopotamia, while Chinese cargo ships called 'junks' are known to have travelled as far as Africa.

The ancient Greek navy

- **Ever since they were first developed,** ships have played an important role in times of both war and peace. However, the vast differences between these two roles led to the manufacture of vessels solely for warfare.

- **As maritime trade flourished** in ancient times, neighbouring countries began to compete with each other for dominance. As the existing merchant vessels were inadequate for battles at sea, they started to build warships.

- **The Phoenicians** were the first to develop a war galley. However, the most advanced and practical warships were built by the ancient Greeks, who revolutionized the art of naval warfare.

- **The war galleys** of the Phoenicians were sailing ships with oars that could be manoeuvred even in the absence of wind.

- **The Greeks** went one step further and equipped their galleys with a bronze-tipped spike. This spike could ram into enemy ships and sink them.

- **The first war galley** to use the spike was the penteconter, a fast vessel with 50 oars. A penteconter was about 35 m long.

- **About 700BC,** the penteconter gave way to the bireme. This war galley had two levels of oarsmen, which gave the ship more power without the need to lengthen it.

> **. . . FASCINATING FACT . . .**
> In the 7th century AD, the Byzantines developed a
> flamingsubstance that could be catapulted at enemy ships
> to set them afire. This substance was known as Greek Fire.

- **As with other ships of its kind**, the oars on the lower level of the bireme were cut into the side of the vessel. However, the second level of oarsmen rowed from the deck.

- **The success of the bireme** eventually led to the creation of the trireme. This was the most effective warship of the time. It had three levels of oarsmen, with as many as 170 oarsmen in one ship.

- **The Greeks used triremes** to devastating effect in the Graeco-Persian wars. The triremes were invincible and played a major part in establishing Greece as a naval power.

▼ *All triremes were named after female mythological characters.*

The ancient Roman navy

- **The earliest Roman navy,** first established about 311BC, was not a very powerful one. The Romans took pride in land warfare and the small navy they had was under the control of the army.

- **Their navy** mainly consisted of a few triremes, which were larger than the Greek ones. But even this small navy was decommissioned a few years later.

- **The Romans developed** a powerful navy about 261BC during the First Punic War against Carthage. But by that time the powerful triremes had lost their place as the dominant warships. So, the Roman navy had to find new ways of countering their enemies.

- **The Roman navy** did not have any experience in building ships. Hence, they based the design of their vessels on quadriremes and quinqueremes captured from Carthage.

- **Contrary to popular belief,** quadriremes and quinqueremes did not have four and five levels of oarsmen. Instead, they probably had one or two rows of oars, with four or five men rowing each oar.

- **These ships** often carried about 100 soldiers and stone-throwing catapults to attack port towns.

- **The Romans** also developed a device called the *corvus*. This was a raised board with a spike on the underside.

- **The *corvus*** was used to board enemy ships. Once on board, the superior Roman infantry easily defeated the enemy.

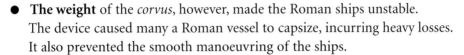
- **The weight** of the *corvus*, however, made the Roman ships unstable. The device caused many a Roman vessel to capsize, incurring heavy losses. It also prevented the smooth manoeuvring of the ships.

- **The Roman navy** was very innovative and some of its strategies are followed even today. The Romans also built harbours at strategic points.

▼ *The ancient Romans often recreated gladiator battles. However, these naval battles were extremely expensive to stage, so they took place only rarely.*

Viking voyagers

- **Vikings** came from the Scandinavian countries of Denmark, Sweden and Norway. They were great travellers and spent much of their life at sea. They also invaded several countries.

- **The name 'Viking'** means 'pirate raid' in the Norse language. Although some Vikings were indeed pirates, most of them were farmers who sailed from their countries in search of better agricultural lands.

- **Their passion** for sailing made the Vikings the best shipbuilders of their time. They built two kinds of ships, the longship and the *knarr*.

- **The longship** was a long, narrow vessel, mainly used as a warship. The longship was about 30 m long, and was powered by a single, square sail.

- **The sails** were made of sheep's wool or linen and often cost more than the rest of the ship.

- **Viking women** were responsible for making the sails. They first made small, diamond-shaped pieces and trimmed them with leather strips. These pieces were then sewn together to make a large, square sail.

- **The *knórr*** was a heavy cargo ship. It was about 17 m long and wider than the longship. It was used to carry cargo, such as wool, timber, grain and even livestock.

- **When building a ship**, the Vikings first erected the keel, a large beam around which the hull of the ship was built. The keel ran the entire length of the ship, from the bow to the stern, and was made of a single piece of wood.

- **Wooden planks** were affixed to the sides of the keel in an overlapping pattern. The planks were then fastened with iron nails. This technique made the ships sturdy and flexible. The floor was set on the keel, and bars were put across to make a deck and seats for oarsmen. The ships were steered by oars at the stern.

- **The bow** of the longship sometimes had an ornate carving of a snake or a dragon head. These ships, therefore, were often referred to as 'dragon ships' by the Vikings' enemies.

◀ *Viking ships are believed to be the first vessels to have crossed the Atlantic Ocean. The Vikings discovered Iceland around AD860 and settled in the new land.*

Christopher Columbus

- **Christopher Columbus** (1451–1506) was an Italian explorer who sailed across the Atlantic Ocean to establish a westward sea route to Asia. Instead, this great mariner landed in the Americas.

- **Columbus** was only 14 years old when he first set out to sea. He worked on various ships and even led voyages to Tunisia and Anjou in Africa.

- **After settling in Portugal** for a few years, Columbus moved to Spain with his son. Columbus was driven by a passion for exploring new lands. He made repeated pleas to the Spanish monarchs to fund his expeditions.

- **Initially**, Columbus received no support. The Christian rulers of Spain were more concerned with battling the Moorish kingdom of Granada, than with funding overseas exploration. However, once victory against Granada became certain, they became more receptive.

- **Columbus** once again approached King Ferdinand and Queen Isabella of Spain. This time he convinced them that he would find a trade route to the Far East.

- **On August 3, 1492**, the Italian mariner finally set sail from Palos, Spain with three ships, *Niña*, *Pinta* and *Santa Maria*. The ships carried over 100 men, ship repairing equipment and other supplies.

- **After sailing** for five long months, Columbus and his crew sighted land. They set foot on an island that they thought was in Asia. But it was actually a part of the Bahamas. Columbus named this island San Salvador.

- **Columbus** continued his journey to Cuba, Haiti and the Dominican Republic. He named the natives 'Indians', since he thought that he was, in fact, in the Indies.

- **On March 15, 1493**, Columbus returned to Spain, where he was accorded a hero's welcome. He was given the title of Admiral of the Ocean Seas and made the governor of all the lands he had discovered.

- **Convinced that Asia** was located beyond the islands he had discovered, Columbus made three more trips to the west between 1493 and 1502. During this period he discovered Jamaica, Trinidad and Tobago, Grenada, Venezuela and Central America.

◀ Santa Maria *was wrecked when it ran into rocks off the coast of present-day Haiti. Its remains were used to build a fort on the island.*

Vasco da Gama

- **Vasco da Gama** (c. 1460–1524) was a Portuguese explorer who discovered a sea route to India.

- **In 1488**, Bartolomeu Dias had opened up the possibilities of a new route to the East by discovering the southern tip of Africa. He established that India could be reached by water, but his work was only half done.

- **Arab traders** held the monopoly of trade with the Eastern countries at that time. In order to outflank them, King João II of Portugal commissioned Estevão da Gama, Vasco's father, to complete Dias' journey.

- **Estevão** died before he could complete the voyage. Moreover, a shortage of funds put an end to further Portuguese expeditions for a brief period.

- **Following the death** of King João II in 1495, his cousin, King Manuel I ascended the throne of Portugal. King Manuel I decided to renew João's efforts to reach the East and put Vasco da Gama in charge of the expedition.

- **Vasco da Gama** planned his journey thoroughly and stocked four ships with supplies. He was accompanied by Goncalo Alvares, his brother Paolo da Gama and his companion Nicolao Coelho, who often sailed with Vasco da Gama.

- **On July 8, 1497**, da Gama set sail from Lisbon. His crew consisted of 170 men, many of whom were convicts.

- **By December**, Vasco da Gama's fleet had reached the southernmost part of Africa. From there, the fleet continued to sail along the east coast of Africa.

- **Vasco da Gama** stopped at coastal towns like Mozambique and Mombassa to replenish his stocks. Throughout his journey he faced opposition from Arab traders. Vasco, however, met an Arab guide at Malindi, in what is now Kenya. The guide agreed to lead the Portuguese across the Arabian Sea.

● **On May 20, 1498**, Vasco da Gama finally reached the Indian port of Calicut, which was then the main trading centre for spices and precious stones.

◄ *In 1524, Vasco da Gama was made the Portuguese viceroy to India and he set off on his third and final voyage. This great explorer, however, died soon after arriving in the city of Cochin, India.*

Ferdinand Magellan

- **Ferdinand Magellan** was born in 1480, into a noble Portuguese family. He led the first sea voyage around the globe. He was also the first European to cross the Pacific Ocean.

- **Like Columbus**, Magellan believed that a westward sea passage to Asia existed. He also realized that he would need to cross the New World, or the Americas, to do so.

- **Having fallen** out of favour with of the Portuguese monarch, Magellan gave up his nationality and left for Spain. There he approached King Charles I and told him of his plans to approach the Spice Islands in Asia from the west.

- **The king** granted him funds and on September 20, 1519, Magellan set sail with a fleet of five ships and over 200 men. He sailed along the coast of Africa towards Brazil.

◄ *Magellan's journey not only proved that the Earth was round, but also showed that the oceans of the world were linked.*

122

- **On December 6**, Magellan sighted Brazil. After stocking up on suppliesat Rio de Janeiro, the crew continued down the coast of South America towards the Pacific Ocean.

- **Finally**, in October, 1520, they found a strait. Magellan named it the Strait of All Saints. Later this strait was renamed Magellan's Strait.

- **Conditions** in the strait were so difficult that one of the ships turned back. It took the remaining ships nearly 40 days to cross the narrow strait. At night, the crew saw an island where fires from Indian camps glowed through the dark. The crew named this island Tierra del Fuego, meaning 'land of fire'.

- **It took the fleet** four months to cross the Pacific Ocean. During this time, members of the crew suffered because of the lack of food and fresh water. Many came down with scurvy. Finally, the fleet arrived at the island of Guam in the South Pacific, where it managed to stock up on supplies.

- **The crew** continued to sail. On March 28, 1521, they reached the Philippines, where Magellan was killed in a tribal war. However, his crew carried on with the voyage under the leadership of Sebastian del Cano, one of Magellan's most skilled navigators.

- **On May 1, 1521**, Sebastian del Cano arrived at Moluccas, or the Spice Islands. After stocking up on valuable spices, del Cano and his men began their return voyage. Finally on September 6, 1522, one ship carrying 18 crew members arrived in Spain, becoming the first to circumnavigate the globe.

Sir Francis Drake

- **Englishman Sir Francis Drake** (c. 1540–1596) was a skilled navigator. His remarkable achievements demonstrated the growing power of the English navy, which was competing with Spain and Portugal to gain a monopoly over international trade.

- **Drake** commanded his first ship in 1567 and travelled to the Caribbean on a slave-trading mission. During this expedition his fleet was ruthlessly attacked by the Spaniards. After suffering huge losses, Drake set out to replenish the stolen goods.

- **In 1572**, Drake led another expedition. On reaching the Isthmus of Panama, the land liking the Atlantic and Pacific Oceans, Drake became the first Englishman to see the Pacific Ocean. He also led some journeys to the Caribbean, attacking the Spanish ports there.

- **In 1577**, Drake was secretly sent by Queen Elizabeth I to capture the Spanish colonies on the western coast of the Americas. He set sail with five ships on December 13.

- **Drake** did not reveal the intended destination to his crew. When he turned south from Brazil, he faced opposition from his crew members.

- **Drake** disposed of two unfit ships at Rio de la Plata in present-day Argentina. He also gave a remarkable speech to cheer up his crew, and renamed his ship the *Golden Hind*.

- **The journey** proved to be difficult. When the fleet entered the Pacific Ocean after crossing the dangerous strait between the South American landmass and Tierra del Fuego, a violent storm destroyed one ship. Another turned back to England.

- **Drake**, however, did not give up. He continued to sail north, hoping to find a passage through the Americas. It is believed that Drake must have crossed California and reached the United States–Canada border.

- **Unable to find** a passage through the Americas, Drake turned west towards the Pacific Ocean. He visited Moluccas, Celebes, Java and finally the Cape of Good Hope.

- **When Drake** returned home to England in September 1580, he had become the first Englishman to have sailed around the world.

▲ *Queen Elizabeth I visited Drake aboard the* Golden Hind *and knighted him for his efforts.*

125

The Spanish Armada

◀ *On its return voyage, the Armada ran into terrible storms. Many ships were wrecked off the rocky coasts of Scotland and Ireland.*

- **The Spanish Armada** was a great fleet launched in 1588 by Philip II of Spain to invade England and overthrow the queen, Elizabeth I.

- **Commanded by the duke of Medina-Sidonia,** the Armada comprised about 130 ships, largely Spanish. Some ships were from Portugal and Naples.

- **The preparation of the Armada** had actually begun in 1586, under the command of marqués de Santa Cruz. But the English troops commanded by Sir Francis Drake managed to attack Cádiz in 1587 and destroy over 30 ships docked at the harbour.

126

- **The huge fleet** finally set sail for England on May 28, 1588 with 30,000 men aboard. It was the largest fleet ever to be launched at the time and was considered invincible.

- **In July 1588**, an English fleet commanded by Lord Charles Howard engaged the Armada near Plymouth.

- **The battle** between the Armada and the English fleet continued for a week, but the English were unable to break through the Armada's crescent formation.

- **When the Armada** anchored near Calais, France, Lord Charles Howard ordered some ships to be set on fire and sent them against the huge Spanish fleet, hoping to set them on fire.

- **The English fire ships** caused panic among the Spanish and the Armada's formation broke. The English took advantage of this and moved in for the final assault.

- **On July 29, 1588**, the English fleet finally defeated the Armada in the Battle of Gravelines. About 15,000 Spaniards died in the battle.

- **Due to the terrible storms**, only 67 badly damaged ships of the Armada managed to return home.

...FASCINATING FACT...
Known for their experimentation, the English had equipped around 10,000 of their troops with firearms, while the Spaniards mostly depended on bows and arrows.

Pirate aboard!

▲ *Marooning was a terrible fate. The pirate was left alone while his friends sailed away. He was given a few vital things – a pistol and ammunition, and a bottle of water.*

● **The word 'pirate'** means someone who robs ships at sea. Plutarch, the ancient Greek historian, was the first to define pirates in about AD100. According to him, pirates were people who attacked ships and maritime cities illegally.

- **The practice of piracy** is thousands of years old. One of the first available documents on piracy was a carving on a clay tablet from 1350BC, which described attacks on ships in North Africa.

- **People turned to piracy** for many reasons. Some sailors became pirates after their ships were captured by other pirates, while many became pirates just for the money.

- **Pirates followed** the increase in trade across the world. Many of them established their own empires, and piracy posed a major threat to merchants and trading vessels.

- **Privateering**, which was allowed legally by several countries, also helped the rise of piracy. It was made popular in the 1500s by Sir Francis Drake, the famous British sailor and explorer.

- **Privateers were given** a special license to attack pirate ships. But many privateers realized they could be wealthier if they became pirates instead.

- **The late 1600s to the early 1700s** marked the peak of piracy. This period, known as the Golden Age of Piracy, saw pirates flourish in the Mediterranean, Europe, Africa, Asia and the Americas.

- **The Island of Nassau** in the Bahamas played an important role during the Golden Age of Piracy. The island served as a resting point for pirates when they returned from their raids.

- **The Golden Age of Piracy** continued until early 1700s, when stern actions, such as torture and death sentences, were taken to suppress piracy.

- **It is believed** that ancient Chinese pirates were extremely organized. They were known to keep records and contracts of all their activities, and even maintained accounts of the payments made by their victims.

Voyages to Australia

- **European sailors** might have found a sea route to the East through the Pacific Ocean. But it was not until the late 1600s that they discovered Australia and New Zealand. However, the maps made after 1540 indicated that a 'southern land' did indeed exist.

- **It is believed** that Chinese traders were in contact with the native inhabitants of this 'southern land', which we now know as Australia.

- **Arabs**, too, are believed to have traded with the natives, later known as Aborigines, in north Australia.

- **Willem Jansz**, a Dutch explorer, was the first European to sight Australia. In 1606, he sailed along 320 km of the Australian coast, all the time under the impression that it was an extension of New Guinea. He called the land Nieu Zelandt. According to certain reports, this name was not adopted. However, another Dutch explorer, Abel Janszoon Tasman, later used it to name New Zealand.

- **The first known landing**, however, took place in 1616. This time another Dutchman, named Dirk Hartog, landed on the west coast of Australia, after his ship was blown off course on route to Java.

- **In 1642**, Abel Tasman explored the southern coast and sighted the island of Tasmania, which was later named after him.

- **William Dampier**, a pirate, was the first Englishman to land in Australia. He explored the northern and western coasts.

- **Captain James Cook** was sent by British royalty in 1768 to discover the east coast of Australia. Sailing on the *Endeavour*, he went around the north coast and sailed along the east coast of the continent.

- **Cook** made a map of the east coast and discovered and named Botany Bay on the southeast of the island continent.

- **In 1786**, the British government decided to colonize Australia. On May 13, 1787, Captain Arthur Phillip of the British Royal Navy set sail for Botany Bay with more than a thousand people, mostly convicts. On January 26, 1788, Captain Phillip established the first European settlement in Port Jackson, what is now Sydney, in Australia. Although the Aborigines initially opposed it, the colonization of Australia was complete by the second half of the 19th century.

▶ *As well as studying the planets, Cook took wildlife experts with him on his explorations. They collected plants that weren't known in Europe, drew sketches and made notes about them.*

Napoleon versus Nelson

- **One of the most** well-known battles in European naval history is the Battle of Trafalgar, fought between a British fleet and the combined fleets of France and Spain.

- **The British fleet** was commanded by Viscount Horatio Nelson. He was appointed commander of the British Mediterranean fleet when war broke out in 1803 between England and France after a brief ceasefire.

- **Nelson's job** was to block French ports so as to stop merchant trade. He was in charge of blocking trade activity at Toulon in France.

- **This blockade** effectivly kept the French from invading Britain. Napoleon Bonaparte, emperor of France, was nurturing ambitions of conquering Britain.

▶ *Horatio Nelson, one of Britain's greatest naval admirals, was blinded in his right eye during a battle in 1794. He also lost his right arm during another battle in 1797.*

- **Frustrated** with the blockade, Bonaparte sent orders to the French navy to break it. The mission was handed over to Charles de Villeneuve of France.

- **He reached Cape Trafalgar** near Cadiz in Spain. Villeneuve formed his ships into a single battle line so as to break open the blockade.

- **Nelson**, however, had different plans. He divided his fleet into two. He then caught Villeneuve completely off-guard by charging at right angles to the line of French and Spanish ships.

- **Villeneuve** was not prepared for this. The British fleet had an easy advantage and demolished the fleet.

- **So masterly** was the plan that the battle was over in a few hours. It began before noon and ended by late afternoon.

- **Nearly 20** French and Spanish ships had been destroyed, and Villeneuve was taken a prisoner along with thousands of others.

...FASCINATING FACT...
Admiral Nelson spent about 30 years at sea and fought bravely in a number of battles. Yet it is believed that there was one problem he could never overcome – his seasickness! He is said to have planned his battles days in advance, so that he had time to adjust to the sea by the time he had to fight.

The Titanic

- The *Titanic* was the pride of the White Star Line, a British shipping company. Built in Belfast, Northern Ireland, the luxury ocean liner was one of the largest passenger steamships of the time.

- **The ship** belonged to company's Olympic-class liners. The others in this line were the *Olympic* and *Britannic*. The *Britannic* sank in 1916 after striking a mine laid by a German submarine in the Aegean Sea.

- **Like all transatlantic liners**, the *Titanic* was meant to transport passengers between Europe and the US. It was about 260 m long and 28 m wide

- **The ship had about 900** crew members and could carry over 3000 passengers. Since the *Titanic* also carried mail, it was categorized as a Royal Mail Steamer, or RMS.

- **The *Titanic*** was the ultimate name in luxury at the time. Its most striking feature, the grand staircase, was immortalized in James Cameron's epic film based on the ship's tragic voyage. The ship had 16 watertight compartments in its hull and was thought to be unsinkable.

◀ *After its collision with an iceberg, the renowned* Titanic *took only three minutes to break apart and start sinking.*

> **...FASCINATING FACT...**
> Violet Constance Jessup, one of the crew members who survived
> the *Titanic* sinking, was aboard all three Olympic-class liners when
> disaster struck. She was a stewardess on the *Olympic* during the
> ship's collision with HMS *Hawke* in 1911. She was a nurse aboard
> the *Britannic* when it sank in the Aegean Sea in 1916.

● **At noon on April 10, 1912**, the *Titanic* began her maiden voyage. She set sail from Southampton, England, towards New York, United States. Among the passengers were several famous personalities including the American businessmen Benjamin Guggenheim and John Jacob Astor IV, and the writers Jacque Futrelle and Francis Davis Millet.

● **Four days later**, on April 14, the ship struck an iceberg off the coast of Newfoundland. It was almost midnight when the disaster occurred.

● **The iceberg** ripped through the hull, causing the first six watertight compartments to flood. Soon, the ship broke in two and the bow sank almost immediately. It was followed by the stern, which hit the ocean bottom at high speed, severely damaging the hull.

● **Another steamship**, called *Californian*, was anchored nearby when the disaster struck. The crew members of the *Californian* had seen the white rockets being fired from the *Titanic*. However, they failed to recognize these as distress signals.

● **By the time** the Cunard liner *Carpathia* came to the rescue, almost 1500 passengers had died. Only 712 passengers lived to tell the story.

Finding the way

- **Marine navigation** involves guiding a boat or ship safely through the waters to its destination.

- **In ancient times**, mariners stayed close to the shore so that they would not lose their way. In such instances, sailors used coastal navigation to determine their position. They kept in sight of land and used landmarks as reference points.

- **When they finally** ventured into the open seas, these early seafarers depended on the positions of the Sun, stars and other celestial bodies to determine directions. Several instruments, including the sextant, were designed for this purpose.

- **Modified versions** of some of the basic navigational tools from yesteryear are still in use. The most well-known is the magnetic compass, which is crucial in determining the direction at sea.

- **A compass consists** of a moving needle that automatically points towards the Earth's magnetic north. The instrument has been in use since the 12th century. The mariner's compass was an early form of the magnetic compass.

> **...FASCINATING FACT...**
> To calculate ship speed, early mariners dropped overboard a log tied to a reel of rope, knotted at regular intervals. The faster the ship travelled, the more the rope was unwound from the reel. The mariners counted the number of knots pulled off the reel in a given period of time and determined the speed of the ship in knots.

- **The mariner's compass** consisted of an iron needle and a lodestone. The needle was rubbed against the lodestone, then stuck in a piece of straw and floated in a bowl of water. The needle would come to a rest pointing towards north.

- **Other primitive tools** of navigation included the jackstaff. This instrument was used to measure the Pole Star's distance from the horizon and thus determine the position of the vessel at sea.

- **Ancient navigators** also used a line with a piece of lead on one end to measure the depth of the water, thereby determining how far into the sea the vessel has sailed.

- **Dead reckoning** was another popular method of determining the position of a vessel. For this, navigators calculate the ship's position, or the 'fix', with its speed, time and direction.

▲ *A sextant is a navigational instrument used to measure the angle and distance between two heavenly bodies such as the Sun and the Earth.*

- **Nautical charts** provided details about bodies of water, like their depth of the water and the location of islands, shores, rocks and lighthouses.

Diving through time

- **The fascination** that humans have for the mysteries of the oceans is not recent. History is full of stories regarding early attempts by ancient adventurers to become great underwater explorers.

- **It is believed** that around the fifth century BC, a man named Scyllias, from the Greek city of Scione, saved the Greeks from Persian attack by diving beneath the sea and cutting off the anchors of the Persian ships.

- **The history of diving** goes back to the time of Alexander the Great. Greek philosopher Aristotle records in his writings that a diving bell was used during Alexander's reign.

- **The diving bell** was the most widely used piece of diving equipment in the early days. Its origins can be traced back to ancient times, when divers placed inverted buckets and cauldrons over their heads before going underwater.

- **These inverted objects** trapped air inside them, allowing the diver to breathe. These devices gradually gave way to a more sophisticated bell-shaped wooden barrel that was placed over the diver's head.

> ... FASCINATING FACT ...
> In his account of the Peloponnesian Wars, the Greek historian, Thucydides, recounts an incident during the Athenian attack on Syracuse, an ally of Sparta. According to Thucydides, the soldiers of Syracuse fixed wooden poles underwater to block entry into the harbour. These unseen poles caused immense damage to Athenian ships. However, Athenian diving warriors removed the poles to clear the way for their ships.

- **Air was passed** into the bell through tubes that went all the way up to the surface. Over the years the bell was made larger to allow for more air.

- **A more advanced version** of the diving bell is still used today. The modern bells are made of steel and can withstand tremendous amounts of pressure.

- **Divers in ancient Rome** were called *urinatores*, derived from the Latin word *urus*, meaning 'leather bag'. They got their name from the leather bag they carried while diving. These divers recovered treasures from sunken ships. They used heavy stones to help them dive to depths of about 30 m.

- **It is said** that around the first century BC *urinatores* salvaged a cargo of amphorae, or ancient wine jars, from the ancient Roman merchant ship, *Madrague de Giens*.

- **Divers** were also a major force in naval battles. According to historical accounts, Alexander the Great had to contend with *kalimboi*, or diving warriors, during the siege of Tyre in 332BC.

▲ *In ancient times, air was passed to the divers through long tubes that went all the way up to the surface.*

139

Underwater fashion

- **Diving suits** have seen many trends over the years. The earliest example is believed to have been made around the fifteenth century. The diver was restricted in how far down he could dive by his air tube, which went up to the surface of the water.

- **It was only in the eighteenth century** that suits giving freedom of movement were first made. Klingert's diving suit, made around 1797, was one such suit. It was the first to be called a diving suit and comprised a coat and trousers made of waterproof leather.

- **In 1819**, German inventor August Siebe made a heavy-footed diving suit using canvas and leather. The unique feature of this invention was a copper helmet that was supplied with air by a surface pump.

- **Modern diving suits** can be broadly divided into soft and hard types. Soft diving suits are primarily used for scuba diving and other styles of diving. These suits protect the diver from low temperature but not high pressure.

- **Hard diving suits** are more appropriate for deep-sea diving. They are armour-like suits that have pressure joints to protect the diver from the high pressure underwater.

- **Soft diving suits** are of two kinds – wet and dry. Wet suits keep the body warm. They trap small amounts of water, which is then warmed by body heat. The warm layer of water in turn keeps the diver warm.

- **Divers entering colder waters**, such as the polar seas, wear dry suits. These are made of a waterproof material that keeps the diver dry. Divers wear special underclothes or use built-in electrical heating to keep warm.

- **Some suits** have a weight belt to help divers stay at the bottom. Head gear is equipped with visors and is made of the same material as the suit.

140

- **Another invention** that revolutionized diving is the rebreather. Invented by Henry Fleuss, an English marine officer, in 1879, this portable air supply system in the form of tanks freed divers from the constant dependence on air supplied from the surface. This was the first self-contained underwater breathing apparatus, abbreviated to scuba.

- **The invention** of the aqualung by Jacques Cousteau and Emile Gagnan in 1942 further popularized diving. A high-pressure cylinder, worn on the diver's back, is connected to the mouth with a hose that has a valve.

▲ *Divers control their breathing to make their oxygen supply last as long as possible.*

141

Ships today

- **Modern ships** and boats have come a long way when compared to those used in ancient times. Today, we have a wide choice of ships and boats suited for all purposes, from pleasure boats to cargo ships and battleships.

- **The sailboats** of yesteryear have given way to sophisticated fuel-driven vessels. Iron, steel and fibreglass hulls have replaced wooden hulls to provide greater speed and durability.

- **Modern commercial ships** are of various types. However, they are broadly classified into cargo and passenger ships. Cargo ships are used to transport goods, while passenger liners carry people.

- **Among the different kinds** of cargo ships, tankers are most widely used. These ships are used to transport crude oil, petroleum or chemicals, and are the largest ocean-going vessels.

- **Reefers**, or refrigerated container ships, are used for transporting perishable goods, such as fruit, vegetables and meat.

- **Boats**, too, are of different types. These include high-speed jet boats, motorboats, iceboats, rowboats and sailboats.

- **Oars and sails** are still extremely popular. However, motorboats are more common now. These vessels have an internal-combustion engine that provides both speed and power.

- **Modern navies** have a variety of warships. These include cruisers, destroyers, aircraft carriers, frigates and various support vessels.

- **Our knowledge** of marine life and resources depends heavily on research vessels. Fitted with state-of-the-art equipment, these ships undertake study expeditions.

▲ *Frigates are an important part of modern navies. They are used to protect trading ships as well as other warships. They are also a major constituent of anti-submarine warfare.*

● **Specialized ships** and boats are used for fishing, patrolling, repairing and rescue operations. Sophisticated vessels like trawlers, long liners, seiners and lobster boats that use a variety of fishing gear have replaced old wooden fishing boats.

143

Modern navigation

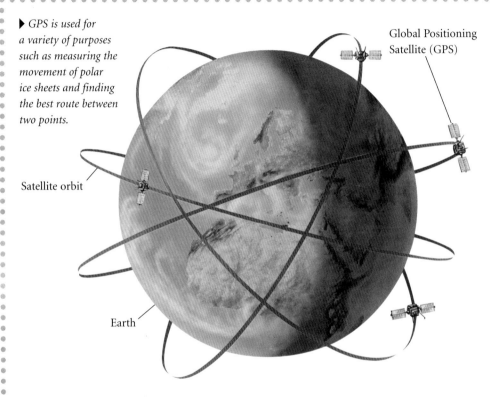

▶ *GPS is used for a variety of purposes such as measuring the movement of polar ice sheets and finding the best route between two points.*

Global Positioning Satellite (GPS)

Satellite orbit

Earth

- **The navigation equipment** used in the early days of seafaring has undergone a major change. Electronic navigation has replaced manual techniques, and advanced high-tech gadgets are now being used worldwide.

- **Modern navigational tools** provide data that are more accurate than ancient, manual methods. Some of the most important inventions are radio direction finding, long-ranging navigation and radar.

- **One of the first forms** of radio navigation was radio direction finding, or RDF. With this method, navigators tuned in to a particular radio frequency to determine their position. Some signals also had their own Morse code.

- **Long-range navigation**, or Loran, helps to fix the position of the ship by measuring the time taken by different radio signals to reach the receiver from fixed onshore transmitters.

- **The most popular form** of Loran is Loran-C, which uses two land transmittors simultaneously. This system is now being replaced by the global positioning system, or GPS.

- **GPS is a type of modern** satellite navigation, or satellite positioning system. This process uses 24 artificial satellites orbiting the Earth, the first of which was launched in the early 20th century.

- **With this system**, the navigator has a GPS receiver. A control device keeps track of the satellites, which send signals and the exact time. Comparing data from more than one satellite, the receiver calculates the ship's position.

- **The traditional** dead-reckoning system (DRS) has been modified into the inertial guidance system. This has the same function as the earlier DRS, but is more accurate.

- **Radio detection and ranging**, popularly called radar, is another commonly used navigational technique. Radar helps to locate faraway objects by bouncing radio waves off them.

- **A radar uses a scanner** to determine the location of objects, and has a display that shows its findings. It can not only locate the presence and position of an object but also determine its shape, size, speed and direction of movement.

Modern cargo ships

▲ *Cargo ships that have fixed routes and charges are known as liners. Tramps are ships that do not operate on any definite route or schedule. These vessels arrive at any port where cargo is available.*

● **Cargo ships**, also called freighters, are usually huge and are used to transport cargo such as cars, trucks, food products, petroleum, textiles, minerals, gas and metals.

● **There are two main kinds** of cargo ships – container ships and bulk carriers. Tankers and supertankers are also cargo ships, but considered a separate category due to the nature of their cargo.

- **Container ships** carry their cargo in large containers. They are sometimes referred to as 'box boats'. These ships carry all kinds of dry cargo, from computers and televisions to furniture and foodstuffs.

- **Bulk carriers** are single deck vessels that are used to carry unpackaged, free-flowing dry cargo, such as grain, ore and coal. These ships have one large container or space. Products such as grain and coal are poured into this large container through openings in its roof.

- **Small container ships** called 'coasters' carry small amounts of cargo from minor ports to major ports. They are also known as feeder vessels, since they 'feed' cargo to bigger container ships.

- **Coasters** are named after the fact that they travel along the coast. These ships usually make more than one stop per trip.

- **With the advent** of container ships, huge cranes became a standard feature at cargo ship docks. Some cargo ships have onboard cranes called derricks. Cranes and derricks speed up the process of loading and offloading cargo.

- **Roll-on-roll-off**, or RORO vessels, and lighter aboard ships, or LASH, are popular alternatives to container ships. RORO ships have openings on their sides and stern, or the back of the ship, through which cars, trucks and even wheeled containers can be driven aboard.

- **The LASH vessel** is also called a barge carrier. It is a long cargo ship with a crane mounted on its deck. In this system, cargo is placed in flat-bottomed boats, or barges, that are loaded into a mothership, or LASH carrier.

- **The vessel** can load or offload several barges near a port and move on without wasting time. Barges that have been left behind are towed into the docks and offloaded at leisure.

Tankers

- **Tankers** are huge ships used for transporting petroleum or natural gas. Some tankers also carry chemicals.

- **All countries** depend on oil and oil products, but few have these natural resources. Oil therefore needs to be transported from oil-rich countries to other parts of the world.

- **Oil pipelines** and tankers are the only two modes of transporting oil around the world. Tankers are, in fact, one or more tanks designed like a ship.

- **Tankers are divided** into various groups depending upon the nature of their cargo. The different types of tankers include Liquid Natural Gas (LNG) carriers, Very Large Crude Carriers (VLCC), Ultra Large Crude Carriers (ULCC), Medium Range carriers, SUEZMAX and PANAMAX.

▼ *Some tankers have caused huge environmental damage. Oil spills and other accidents can adversely affect the environment and marine life.*

- **The largest** of all tankers are the supertankers. They are alternatively known as VLCCs or ULCCs. These tankers are about 400 m long and mainly carry crude oil.

- **Supertankers** are bigger than even aircraft carriers, making them the biggest ships in the world. Since they are too large to approach most ports, these ships often have to offload their cargo into smaller vessels. Today, however, some ports have deepwater offloading facilities that are connected to the mainland by pipelines.

- **Tankers** carry millions of litres of oil. Even the smallest accident can cause the oil to spill and result in extensive damage to the environment. Hence, tankers require extremely strong hulls to prevent such accidents.

- **Tankers** with single hulls are at the most risk, since the hull is also the wall of the oil tanks. A breach in the hull would lead to a major oil spill.

- **Double-hulled tankers** are now becoming the norm. These vessels are considered safer because there is a space between the hull and the tanks.

- **Tankers** also have sophisticated fire-fighting equipment, along with modern pumps to load and offload their liquid cargo.

> **FASCINATING FACT**
> The Norwegian-operated tanker, the *TT Jahre Viking*, formerly known as *Seawise Giant*, is the largest ship in the world. It is 458 m long and 69 m wide.

Container ships

- **In the 1950s,** Malcolm Mclean, an American trucker, came up with an alternative for the time-consuming and expensive process of manually loading and offloading cargo.

- **McLean** suggested that ships be loaded with big ready-made containers. These containers would be filled with cargo and lifted by cranes onto ships directly from trucks.

- **This process** of using containers to carry cargo is called 'containerization'. It is believed that the idea struck Mclean while waiting for the cargo from his truck to be loaded onto a ship.

- **Container shipping** integrated the movement of goods from trucks, trains, ships and even planes. Today, almost 90 percent of the world's cargo is moved in containers.

- **The first container ship** was the *Ideal X*, which sailed from New Jersey in 1956. The world's first terminal exclusively for containers was constructed in Port Elizabeth, New Jersey.

- **The OOCL SX-class vessels** are the world's largest container ships. The first to be built, the *Shenzhen*, is 323 m long and over 40 m wide. The vessel was launched on April 30, 2003.

- **Over the years,** container ships have also been modified to better suit the products they carry. Some carry sophisticated refrigerated containers for transporting perishable commodities such as fish, meat and fruit. These are called refrigerated ships, or 'reefers'.

- **Reefers** contain heavily insulated compartments. These ships have several locker spaces that can carry different products at a variety of temperatures. The cargo is moved about on conveyor belts or by electric fork-lift trucks.

- **Reefer equipment** has been modified to keep the goods they carry as fresh as possible. Most reefer containers have their own refrigeration units, which can be plugged into the ship's power source. If necessary, some reefers can even provide a humid environment for protecting sensitive products from dehydration.

- **Some reefers** are used to transport medicines, while others are used to keep goods from freezing in harsh climates.

▲ *Cargo is loaded onto container ships by huge cranes that can lift 20–30 containers per hour.*

Fishing vessels

- **People have used boats** for fishing since the beginning of civilization. Commercial fishing may be carried out by a single fisherman who takes his boat out to sea, or by huge fishing fleets.

- **Fishermen** in some countries still go out to sea in small wooden boats to cast their nets and wait for the catch. However, traditional fishing boats and methods have given way to bigger, more advanced vessels and new techniques that produce a very large haul.

- **There are three main** fishing vessels that can be found across the world. These are trawlers, seiners and long liners. All these vessels are more than 40 m long.

- **Trawlers,** also known as 'draggers', drag heavy nets, called trawls, across the seabed or through the water. These vessels are mainly used to catch shrimp, salmon and other edible marine creatures.

- **Whereas earlier trawlers** had sails, the modern ones are powered by diesel. They are often large and can measure up to 120 m in length.

▶ *Trawlers also have refrigeration facilities, allowing them to keep the catch fresh. Hence these vessels can also stay out at sea for several days.*

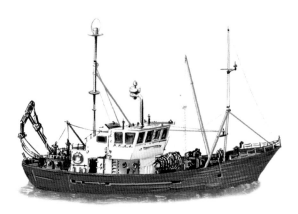

- **Unlike trawlers,** the mouths of seiner nets are closed before hauling them aboard. Seiners target fast-swimming fish like tuna and herring. The nets are allowed to float on water to catch these fish.

- **Long-liners** do not use nets at all. Instead, they have long lines with numerous baited hooks along their length. These lines trail behind the ship, hooking tuna, cod and even small sharks.

- **Other less common** fishing vessels include shrimp or lobsters boats, head boats and dive boats.

- **The sophistication** of modern fishing vessels has created its own problems. The use of modern equipment has increased the size of the catch but not without greatly reducing the fish populations in many regions. Most countries now regulate hauls in order to prevent the decrease in fish populations.

...FASCINATING FACT...
'Bycatch' is a term used to describe sea creatures that are not meant to be caught but are trapped inadvertently in fishing nets. Often the bycatch is not returned to the water despite the fact that it is unsuitable for commercial use.

Luxurious liners

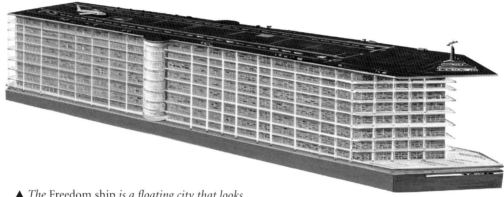

▲ *The* Freedom ship *is a floating city that looks like an enormous barge. It has its own casino, hotel units, a school – the students of which can visit a different country every week – and business units.*

- **Ships in ancient times** were not only used to carry goods, but were also a popular mode of transportation for people. Until the invention of the aeroplane, ships were the only way that people could cross the seas to new lands.

- **Ships that carry people** are called 'passenger ships'. These can vary in sizes. Smaller vessels are used for short, coast-to-coast journeys, while large ships with lavish amenities, called cruise ships, are used for pleasure trips.

- **Cruise ships** appeared only towards the latter half of the 20th century. Before that, intercontinental voyages were undertaken in large, motorized ships known as ocean liners.

- **Ocean liners** thrived towards the end of 19th century, when millions of people each year were emigrating from Europe to the United States. Some of the most famous ocean liners are the *Titanic, Mauretania, Normandie* and *Lusitania*.

- **The increased use** of ocean liners led to the establishment of several shipping companies. The better known of these included the White Star Line and the Cunard line.

- **The Cunard Line** is a British company that today owns the famous cruise ships, *Queen Elizabeth 2* and *Queen Mary 2*. It was set up by Samuel Cunard, the Canadian shipping pioneer, who along with a few others formed the British and North American Royal Mail Steam Packet Company.

- **The Cunard Line** was the first regular steamship service between Europe and the United States. Two huge Cunard liners, *Mauretania* and *Lusitania*, were launched in 1906. They were both around 240 m long. The latter was sunk by a German submarine in 1915.

- **The Cunard liners** were not the fastest or the largest. In fact, the company's rivals, the White Star Line, owned the fastest ships of that time. However, Cunard ships were known for their safety, which set the company apart.

- **World War I** severely disrupted the transatlantic service. Some liners were taken over and used to transport troops. After the war, the transatlantic services recovered and boomed.

- **France launched the *Normandie***, a liner famous for its luxury and modern art. Cunard followed with the launch of the *Queen Mary*, which was 310 m long. The revival, however, did not last long. World War II and the advent of jet aeroplanes in the 1950s put an end to the transatlantic ocean liners.

Ferries

- **Ferries** usually have fixed routes, schedules and destinations. They most commonly operate from towns and cities near rivers and seas, and are an important means of public transport.

- **They mainly run** across rivers or bays, or from one point in a harbour to another. Long-distance ferries connect coastal islands with each other, or with the mainland.

- **The Staten Island Ferry** in the New York City harbour is a famous harbour ferry. The most well known long-distance ferry operates in the English Channel, between Great Britain and the rest of Europe.

- **Large ferries** also operate between Finland and Sweden. Some of these ferries carry hundreds of cars in their car decks, and even transport railcars.

- **When a ferry** makes several stops it is called a waterbus. Such motorized vessels are common across the major water channels of Venice, Italy.

- **Ferry boats dock** at a specially designed ferry slip. If the ferry transports vehicles, the slip usually has an adjustable ramp called an 'apron' to facilitate loading and unloading.

- **Many ferry services** in Europe use hydrofoils, which are boats with wing-like foils mounted on struts below the hull. As the vessel picks up speed, the foils lift the hull out of water. This ensures a speedy service.

- **The Spirit of Tasmania** ferries form one of the best-known ferry services in the world. It carries passengers and vehicles across the Bass Strait between Tasmania and mainland Australia.

- **The world's largest ferry** operations can be found in the Strait of Georgia in British Columbia, Canada and Puget Sound in Washington, United States. Each operation comprises about 25 ferries.

▲ *A ferry is a boat or a ship that transports passengers over short distances. Some also carry vehicles and animals.*

Tugs and icebreakers

- **Tugs, or tugboats**, are small but extremely powerful motorized ships. They are mainly used to guide ships into the docks. They also tow defective ships, barges and heavy equipment across open seas.

- **Although they are known** as tugboats, these are actually small ships and are quite strong despite their size. Modern tugs have diesel engines and can move at a reasonably good speed of 20 km/h.

- **Tugs are also used** to haul oil rigs to new locations. In addition, they can steer huge tankers in and out of oil ports.

- **Tugboats** can be divided into two main groups: habour tugs and ocean-going tugs. Harbour tugs, or short-haul tugs, are used to move ships in the vicinity of the harbour.

- **Ocean-going**, or long-haul, tugs are used to salvage ships from open seas and guide them to the dockyards for repair, or to tow floating docks and rigs to different locations.

- **Dredgers** are ships that collect sand and other sediments from the seabed. They are often used to deepen channels in harbours to prevent them from getting blocked. The material that is scooped up is used for commercial purposes.

- **Icebreakers** are tough, specialized vessels that are used to clear ice in rivers and seas in order to create a passage.

- **They are very sturdy** and usually quite heavy. They have an armoured body to withstand shocks experienced during collisions with ice.

- **They ram into ice sheets**, or masses of hard ice, and shatter them. Sometimes they crack open an ice sheet by weighing it down with their sheer bulk.

- **Icebreakers** help clear the way so that ships can follow. They are also used for exploration in the polar regions.

▼ *Tugboats are powerful ships and are used to guide ships, such as this aircraft carrier, to new locations.*

Submersibles and tenders

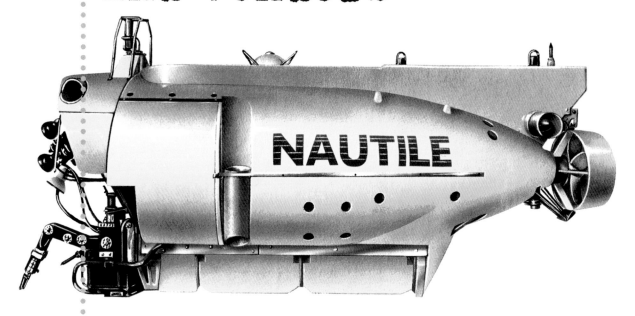

▲ *The submersible,* Nautile, *made more than 90 dives into the ocean depths to recover artefacts from the ill-fated* Titanic.

- **Specialized vessels** such as submersibles, tugboats, icebreakers and dredgers often lend ships a helping hand and perform tasks that other ships are unable to perform.

- **The submersible** is an underwater research vessel. It is primarily used to conduct underwater scientific research and for military and industrial purposes.

- **Submersibles** aid in studies of undersea geological activity, marine life, and mineral deposits. They also help to check on oil rigs. Submersibles involved in research usually accompany a huge research vessel.

- **Navies** use submersibles for a variety of tasks, including submarine rescue and repair, and mine detection.

- **Wreck divers** use submersibles for salvage operations, such as recovering ships, planes or valuable equipment that have sunk to the ocean depths.

- **Pressurized submersibles** are designed to operate in very deep waters. They can withstand the high pressure near the seabed.

- **The most sophisticated** of all submersibles are the remotely operated vehicles. These vessels do not need a pilot and are equipped with video and still-cameras and sensors.

- **Tenders are ships or boats** that service other ocean-going vessels. There are various types of tenders, including ships' tenders and submarine tenders. Tenders of smaller boats are called dinghies.

- **A ship's tender** helps to transport people or supplies to and from the shore or another ship. A submarine tender is a ship that carries supplies like food, fuel and other equipment to submarines. However, these are not very common nowadays.

- **Some modern cruise liners** have lifeboat tenders. In addition to serving as tenders, they also act as lifeboats. These vessels are bigger than normal lifeboats.

Battleships

▲ Chih Yeun, *the mighty Chinese battlecruiser, was one of the heaviest and most dreaded battleships of its time.*

- **Battleships** dominated navies in the first half of the 20th century. They were large and heavily armoured ships that carried powerful guns.

- **Historically**, the name 'battleships' referred to the line-of-battle ships used during the age of sail, about 1571–1862.

- **During the age of sail,** ships carried heavy cannons, most of which were placed on the sides of the vessel. Since these cannons could only fire straight, the ships fell into lines, one behind the other. This popular battle formation was called the line of battle.

- **Battleships** were rated according to the number of guns they carried. First-rate ships had three decks with over 100 guns, while second-rate ships carried about 90 guns. Third-rate ships, with about 60 guns, were rated the lowest. At times, fourth-rate ships also carried guns.

- **Battleship design** underwent major changes during the 19th century. Wooden sail ships were heavily armoured and refitted with steam engines. Turreted guns were also first used during this period. This helped to considerably reduce the number of guns onboard.

- **Towards the end of the 19th century,** battleship design had become stable and one single design was being followed across the world. Most ships in this period had two turrets, four 12-inch guns and smaller, secondary guns. These ships travelled at a maximum speed of 18 knots.

- **By the end of the 19th century**, ships resembling modern battleships started to appear, beginning with HMS *Devastation* and HMS *Thunderer*.

- **Countries** started to spend a lot of resources on building more and more powerful battleships. Although dreadnoughts came to the fore during World War I, the typical battleships were back in action in World War II.

- **Well-known battleships** deployed in World War II were the *Bismarck*, the *Misssouri*, the *Prince of Wales* and the *Yamato*.

- **Before the start of World War II**, battleships were the rulers of the seas. However, in World War II they became secondary to aircraft carriers, which offered greater effective range of attack than the battleships.

- **Several battleships** were decommissioned after World War II. Those retained were largely used as escorts to aircraft carriers or for the bombardment of shores. Even these were eventually scrapped in the 1990s.

163

Aircraft carriers

▲ *Most modern aircraft carriers are powered by nuclear energy.*
The heavier and bigger ones can support over 85 planes.

● **Aircraft carriers** are massive warships that carry military aircraft. These ships have flight decks to support the take off and landing of fighters and bombers.

● **Apart from enabling** military planes to take off and land at sea, aircraft carriers also provide air cover to other warships.

● **Most aircraft carriers** have a flat top deck that serves as a strip for take offs and landings. Although it is quite long, it is small compared to normal runways. Hence, steam-powered catapults are used to launch the planes into the air.

- **These catapults** help the planes accelerate from 0 to 240 km/h in just two seconds to attain take off speed.

- **Landing on the carrier** requires great skill. The planes have tailhooks that snag one of four arresting cables stretched across the deck, stopping the aircraft within 100 m.

- **Aircraft carriers** are over 300 m long, with a huge crew. They are expensive, and therefore owned only by a few countries. The United States owns the most carriers. As of 2004, the US Navy has 12 carriers, the most famous being the *Abraham Lincoln.*

- **There are several types** of aircraft carriers, including seaplane tenders, assault carriers, light carriers, escort carriers, fleet carriers and supercarriers. Some of these, such as seaplane tenders, are no longer in use.

- **Most countries today use light carriers**, which can support helicopters and jump jets, or other vertical take off and landing planes. Such aircraft can take off and land with almost no forward movement, and so do not need catapults.

- **Aircraft carriers** are accompanied by many other ships that either provide protection or carry supplies. Together they are called a 'carrier battle group'.

> ...**FASCINATING FACT**...
> American pilot Eugene Fly was the first to take off from a
> stationary ship. He did so from the US cruiser USS
> *Birmingham.* On May 12, 1912, British commander Charles
> Samson became the first pilot to take off from a moving
> warship. He did so from the battleship HMS *Hibernia.*

Submarines

- **Submarines** are warships that operate underwater. Although the term usually refers to military vessels, there are also scientific and commercial submarines. The first submarine was built in 1620 by the Dutch inventor Cornelius Jacobszoon Drebbel. This vessel was propelled using oars.

- **Early submarines** were largely used for underwater exploration. But soon the importance of the submarine as a military vessel was recognized. The first submarine built exclusively for military use was named the *Turtle*.

- **Built in the 1770s**, the *Turtle* was a manually-operated, spherical vessel that could accommodate only one person. Designed by David Bushnell, an American inventor, the *Turtle* was first used during the American War of Independence.

- **Over the next century,** several kinds of submarines were developed. However, they were not put to effective military use until the 20th century. Diesel submarines were first used during World War I.

- **Nuclear-powered submarines** did not enter the scene until well after World War II. With nuclear energy, the vessels could stay submerged for longer periods.

- **The earlier submarines** did not have periscopes. These were added in the mid 19th century. Periscopes offer a view of what's happening above water.

- **Submarines also carry** weapons that include mines, torpedoes, cruise missiles and nuclear-tipped ballistic missiles.

- **Submerging and surfacing** is done with the help of ballast tanks. When a submarine has to dive into the water, its ballast tanks are filled with water. When it needs to resurface, compressed air is forced into the tanks to push out the water.

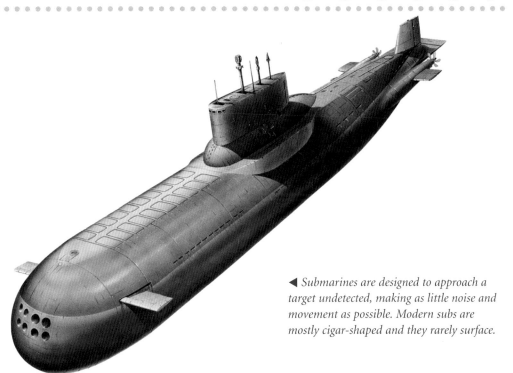

◄ *Submarines are designed to approach a target undetected, making as little noise and movement as possible. Modern subs are mostly cigar-shaped and they rarely surface.*

● **Modern navies** use two basic types of submarines: attack and ballistic missile submarines. Attack submarines are also known as hunter-killer submarines. They usually use torpedoes and are designed to attack warships and other submarines.

● **Ballistic missile submarines** have nuclear warheads to attack land targets such as strategic cities. They are built as back-ups in case all land-based missiles are destroyed.

167

Rowing boats

▲ *Rowing can be categorized into sweeping and sculling. In the first type, each rower uses one oar, while in the latter each rower uses two oars.*

- **Since ancient times,** boats have been used for fun and sporting activities. Such boats include yachts, sailboats, canoes, powerboats and rowing boats.

- **Rowing boats** are moved with oars or paddles. They have been around for centuries. The row boats used for sporting activities consist of a long, slender vessel called a shell. Although shells used to be made from wood, materials such as fibreglass and carbon fibre are more commonly used today.

- **Rowing** east to west across the Atlantic Ocean is tougher than rowing west to east because of ocean currents and so, takes about twice as long.

- **Some rowing boats** are steered by a coxswain, or cox, who sits in the stern, facing the crew. The cox steers the boat and encourages the rowers. Rowing boats that do not have a cox are called 'coxless', or 'straight'.

- **Kayaking and canoeing** have also gained a great deal of popularity in recent years. In both sports, rowers use paddles instead of oars. Unlike oars, paddles are not used in pairs.

- **Both canoes and kayaks** are small vessels that are pointed at the ends. Canoes are mostly open-topped, while kayaks are completely covered, except for an opening for the rower to sit in.

- **Canoes and kayaks** can be paddled by one or more persons. Kayaks have double-ended paddles, while canoes have paddles with single blades. Despite their differences, the word 'canoe' is often used to describe both vessels.

- **There are several sporting competitions** involving canoes and kayaks, including slalom canoeing, rodeo canoeing and canoe polo.

- **Polynesian peoples** once travelled from island to island across the Pacific Ocean in large canoes fitted with outriggers to make them more stable.

....FASCINATING FACT....

Rowing single-handed across the Atlantic Ocean is a tough task. In 1969, an Irish rower managed to make the crossing from west to east in just 70 days.

Sailing ships

- **Sailing ships** use the energy of the wind to move. A sail is made up of pieces of cloth stitched together and tied to long poles called 'masts'.

- **The Egyptians** are believed to have first developed sails. Their reed boats were simple flat-bottomed structures with a huge square sail. Since these vessels did not have a keel, the mast was attached to the edge, or the gunwale, of the boat.

- **The Phoenicians**, during the period 1500–1000BC, modified the sailboats further. They also created a small space in the hull, called the 'deck', to protect sailors from bad weather.

- **New sailing vessels** were developed for use at war. These were known as 'galleys' and had rows of oarsmen as well as sails. These gave way to the bireme, a big vessel that had two decks of oarsmen, followed by the trireme.

- **In China**, shipbuilders built a superior cargo boat called the 'junk'. This boat had a number of sails and was steered by rudders, or movable blades on the stern.

- **The Vikings** developed the longship, which was later replaced by 13th-century cargo vessels, called 'cogs', as the major carrier of goods in Europe.

- **In the 15th century**, sturdy boats called 'caravels' were developed in Spain and Portugal. They had four sails and were up to 25 m in length.

- **Galleons** had long, slender hulls and were quite fast. The Spanish Armada used this vessel. The famous *Mayflower*, which took pilgrims to America in 1620, was a galleon.

- **With the British Empire** beginning to spread its wings in the 19th century, ships became larger and more fortified. They were often used to carry back riches from India and Africa.

● **The advent of steam** ships
gradually led to the demise
of sailing ships. Sailing is
now a leisure activity, and
sailboats are used for
cruising, racing or fishing.

▶ *Egyptian sailboats are called*
fellucas. The earliest record of a ship
under sail is depicted on an Egyptian
pot dating back to 3200BC. These boats
were made of either native woods or
conifers from Lebanon.

Surfing

- **Surfing** involves riding the waves using a surfboard. Surfing is usually done where massive breaking waves are common.

- **Since the 1960s,** the sport has grown in popularity. The dangers involved have only enhanced the excitement and glamour of this sport.

- **Surfers** usually lie on their boards and paddle out to wait for a suitable wave. The idea is to ride a wave as soon as it starts to break.

- **There are several** intricate movements and manoeuvres in surfing. A surfer may ride the crest, or top, of a wave or its breaking curve.

- **The best surfers** can perform manoeuvres in the air. These moves, called aerials, were inspired by skateboarding and snowboarding. In a 360 aerial, a surfer does a 360 degree airborne spin.

- **Surf boards** may be long or short. The longboards are over 2.5 m in length, while shortboards are 2 m or less. Both have small fins to help with stability and steering.

- **Long considered** merely a local recreation, surfing is now an official sport. Professional surfers generally use the shortboard.

- **Surfing** is believed to have originated in Hawaii. Today, it is a highly popular activity worldwide, especially in Australia, South Africa, the United States and Brazil.

- **In competitions,** surfers are judged by the size of the waves and the distance they ride. Skills shown while performing manoeuvres are also considered.

◄ *Surfing requires great strength and agility and lots of practice.*
A good surfer has to be extremely fit and be able to swim well.

Powered for fun

- **With the development of steam** and internal combustion engines in the 1800s, sails and oars became less common and soon motorboats were fashionable. Motorboats are fitted with inboard or outboard motors.

- **Some motorboats** use inboard motors, in which the engine is located within the hull. In outboard motorboats, the motor is attached to the stern of the boat and can be seen at one end.

- **Perhaps the most revolutionary** propulsion system for high-speed was the water-jet engine. In this system, water from under the boat is drawn into a pump-jet and then expelled through an opening at the stern.

- **High-speed boats** are used in search, rescue and salvage operations. They are also used for racing and leisure. Boats like hydroplanes and tunnel boats are especially popular among racing enthusiasts.

- **The streamlined hydroplanes** have projections called sponsons at the front. When a hydroplane picks up speed, it is lifted out of the water and supported by these sponsons.

- **The flat-bottomed tunnel-boat** also has a pair of sponsons, one along each side of the hull. Like the hydroplane, the tunnel boat rises out of the water supported on its sponsons.

- **The runabout** is a high-speed motorboat, which can hold around eight people.

- **Runabouts** can be used for racing but they are more commonly used for fishing and water skiing.

- **Most modern boats** are usually made of plastic and reinforced with fibreglass. These vessels are lightweight, fast and easy to manoeuvre.

- **The most popular** kinds of powerboat racing include jet sprint and offshore powerboat racing. In jet sprint boat racing, boats powered by water-jet propulsion race in shallow watercourses with several sharp turns. Offshore powerboat racing takes place in the open seas.

▲ *Over 14 kinds of high-speed boats are currently used in powerboat racing.*

Riding the waves

- **Water skiing** is another popular water sport. In this, the skier is towed behind a motorboat at great speed. Water skiing can be enjoyed on large, relatively calm expanses of water such as rivers, lakes and bays.

- **The sport** was invented by an American teenager named Ralph Samuelson in 1922. Samuelson believed that it was possible to ski on water as on snow. He chose Lake Pepin in Lake City, Minnesota for his first skiing attempt.

- **A water ski** run begins with the skier crouched low, holding the tow rope attached to the motorboat. Upon acceleration, the skier stands up straight and starts to skim across the surface of the water.

- **Water skis** are made of wood, plastic or fibreglass. They are generally 1.7 m long and 15 cm wide. Unlike snow skis that have a rigid binding for the feet, water skis have rubber mouldings.

- **Today**, there are various categories in water skiing competitions. In the slalom event, the boat runs in a straight line while the skier has to zigzag on one ski around buoys set up in the water. As the skiers successfully complete each run the tow rope is progressively shortened. The skier who completes the course using the shortest rope is the winner.

◀ *Jetskis first went on sale in 1973. They can travel at nearly 100 km/h.*

- **Trick skiing** is performed using either two short skis or a single ski. In this category participants perform tricks, similar to gymnasts, while skiing. Skiers are judged depending upon the difficulty of their tricks and performance.

- **In the jump event**, a pair of long skis is used. Skiers achieve maximum speed before hitting a ramp floating in the water. They use the ramp to launch themselves into the air before falling back into the water again.

▲ *Water skiing is now one of the most popular of all water sports.*

- **Show skiing** involves elaborate preparations. With music and colourful costumes, skiers perform dance acts and ballets. Troupes also form complex human pyramids.

- **Wakeboarding** is an offshoot of waterskiing, which also combines surfing techniques. Instead of skis, the rider stands sideways on a board to 'surf' on the waves created by the boat's wake.

- **Jet skis** are also popular. These are motorized personal watercraft that look like motorbikes and travel at high speeds. Most jet skis can accommodate two or three people. The rider sits or stands on the jet ski.

Oceans in danger

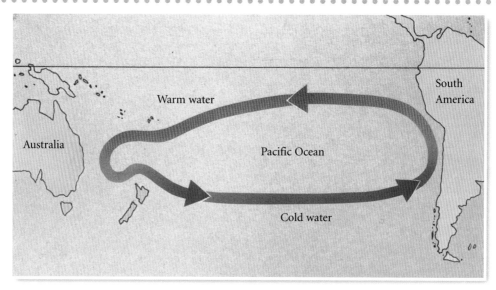

▲ *High atmospheric pressure develops over the Pacific Ocean that causes trade winds to blow from east to west carrying warm surface waters towards the west. This is called the El Niño effect and usually occurs during December.*

- **Oceans**, which occupy about seven-tenths of the Earth's surface, absorb much of the solar heat and are therefore the most affected by global warming.

- **Scientists** believe that the enhanced greenhouse effect could cause more water to be formed due to the melting of glaciers and ice caps than is possible naturally.

- **Global warming** caused by greenhouse gases has increased the Earth's surface temperature by about 0.6°C over the last century.

- **Higher surface temperatures** can melt mountain glaciers and parts of polar ice caps, causing the sea level to go up by a metre within a century or two.

- **This could** have a dangerous effect on the coastlines and the people living in these regions. Many marine species could become extinct if global warming is not checked.

- **El Niño**, a sudden surge of warm waters off the west coast of South America, is a significant climatic phenomenon some scientists attribute to global warming.

- **Oceans** play an important part in controlling the weather. Hence, an increase in their surface temperature will also affect weather patterns. Prolonged drought or increased flooding can wreak havoc on land masses.

- **Global warming** is also responsible for the melting of sea ice and ice caps in the Polar regions. According to recent studies, glaciers along the coast of Greenland are becoming thinner by about one metre every year. The melting of glaciers and sea ice can also increase sea levels, thus reducing coastlines and beaches.

- **Oceans** are considered to be biological pumps for carbon dioxide. They are full of microscopic phytoplanktons, which remove almost half of the natural carbon dioxide formed. Any change in their habitat may lead to further damage, thus directly increasing the amount of carbon dioxide in the atmosphere.

- **Sensing the dangers**, many nations have finally swung into action to save the environment. The Kyoto Protocol, adopted in December 1997, requires the 127 countries that have signed it to take effective measures in order to reduce the amount of greenhouse gases in the atmosphere by 2012.

Greenhouse effect

- **Rapid industrial development** and population growth are taking their toll on the oceans. Some of the factors affecting marine life and the environment include chemical pollution, global warming, oil spills and overfishing.

- **Global warming** is one of the factors that can have an alarming effect on oceans and, thus, life on Earth. The increase in temperature of the Earth's atmosphere and the oceans is called global warming. Some scientists believe that it is the direct result of the greenhouse effect.

- **The Sun's heat** is absorbed by the Earth's atmosphere and radiated back into space. Certain gases in the Earth's atmosphere trap a part of this reflected heat, thus keeping the Earth warm. This process is termed 'natural greenhouse effect'.

- **The greenhouse effect** is similar to what happens in a greenhouse. The surrounding glass allows sunlight in but blocks the heat from going out, thus keeping the temperature warm even when it becomes cold outside.

- **The greenhouse gases** in the atmosphere include water vapour, carbon dioxide, methane, nitrous oxide, ozone and chlorofluorocarbons (CFCs). The amount of greenhouse gases in the atmosphere determines the amount of trapped heat.

- **Water vapour** is the most important greenhouse gas. It is responsible for over 60 percent of the greenhouse effect. Carbon dioxide is the other significant contributor. Chlorofluorocarbons can trap more heat than any other greenhouse gas, but very little of these exist in the atmosphere.

- **Greenhouse gases** in normal quantities are essential, since they provide insulation to the Earth and help sustain life. Industrialization has increased the level of greenhouse gases in the atmosphere, thus trapping more heat than is required. This is called the 'enhanced greenhouse effect'.

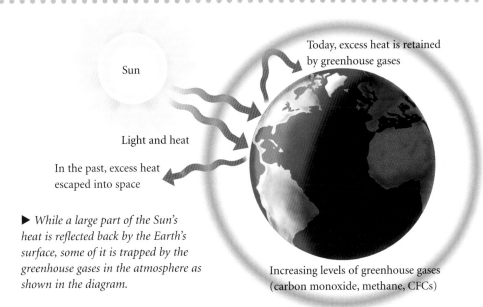

Sun

Light and heat

Today, excess heat is retained by greenhouse gases

In the past, excess heat escaped into space

▶ *While a large part of the Sun's heat is reflected back by the Earth's surface, some of it is trapped by the greenhouse gases in the atmosphere as shown in the diagram.*

Increasing levels of greenhouse gases (carbon monoxide, methane, CFCs)

- **Human activity** has contributed greatly to the increase in the amount of greenhouse gases. The major factor is carbon dioxide emission from fossil fuel combustion.

- **Deforestation** contributes heavily to the increased levels of carbon dioxide in the atmosphere. Trees that have been cut down release carbon dioxide as they decay.

- **Global warming** can cause significant changes in the climatic conditions across the world, thus affecting life on the planet. An increase in temperatures would lead to faster rates of evaporation, the melting of glaciers and polar ice caps, and a rise in sea levels. It would also have an adverse effect on agriculture.

181

Sinking lands

- **The sea level** has already increased rapidly in the last 100 years due to global warming, with many coastal and low-lying areas threatened by flooding.

- **The major reason** for the rise in the level of the sea is the melting of the Arctic and Antarctic ice packs. The thickness of these packs has reduced in the last century, adding to the volume of water in the oceans.

- **Scientists** believe that the level of the oceans will rise more dramatically over the next 100 years, with temperatures expected to rise by almost 4°C.

- **Many major cities** of the world, such as New York, Los Angeles, Rio de Janeiro, London and Singapore, lie in coastal areas or near river mouths.

- **The constant melting** of mountain glaciers and ice packs could threaten these cities with flooding.

- **Scientists** believe that even a 50 cm rise in the sea level will affect millions of people in Bangladesh, India and Vietnam.

- **The population** of small island-states, such as the Seychelles, the Maldives and Tuvalu, will be seriously affected by a rise in the sea level since these countries are only a few metres above it.

- **Tuvalu** is a group of nine coral atolls that lie in the Pacific Ocean, just five metres above sea level. It is predicted that if the present situation continues, then these atolls will be completely submerged within 50 years.

- **Many ecologically sensitive zones**, such as the Everglades in Florida, United States, will become submerged.

- **The rising temperatures** are destroying shallow-water marine life. Global warming is said to be responsible for the destruction of coral reefs in Belize. The Great Barrier Reef off the coast of Australia is also in grave danger.

▼ *The rising sea levels may cause coral reefs, such as the Great Barrier Reef, to become submerged.*

Bleaching the reefs

- **The impact** of global warming on the oceans is most marked in the bleaching of coral reefs.

- **Reefs** are very delicate and sensitive structures, formed by coral polyps. Although polyps feed on passing plankton, their main source of food is the unicellular algae, called 'zooxanthellae', which live within their tissues.

- **The algae feed** on the nitrogen waste produced by the corals. Like all plants, zooxanthellae also produce food using sunlight. It is this that forms the main food of corals.

- **Zooxanthellae** also provide the reefs with their magnificent colouring, which attracts many other marine creatures, thus forming an ecosystem.

- **Reefs** lose colour and die when these zooxanthellae are damaged. This is known as 'bleaching'.

- **Global warming** is the main cause of bleaching. A rise in the temperature of the oceans interferes with the photosynthetic process, eventually poisoning the zooxanthellae. Corals, in turn, are forced to expel the dead zooxanthellae, along with some of their own tissue.

- **Once the algae are expelled**, the corals lose their colour and main source of food. Unless the algae are able to grow again, the corals will gradually starve to death.

> ...FASCINATING FACT...
> Bleaching is dangerous because it affects not only the coral reefs, but also a large number of marine creatures that depend on it for food.

▲ *Like hard corals, non-reef building corals, or soft corals, are also susceptible to bleaching. Soft corals, however, are able to withstand short-term bleaching much more than hard corals.*

- **Widespread bleaching** took place at reefs around Okinawa, Easter Island, and in the Caribbean Sea in 1979 and 1980. The Great Barrier Reef has also undergone bleaching in the last 20 years.

- **Some of the coral reefs** that have been permanently damaged are in the warm waters of the Indian Ocean, including those off the coasts of the Maldives, Sri Lanka, Kenya and Tanzania.

- **Bleached coral reefs** take years to recuperate. Sometimes they get bleached again before they can fully recover from the first attack.

Mineral rich

▶ *Limestone deposits often contain fossils of prehistoric marine creatures.*

- **The oceans** contain an abundant supply of useful minerals. However, their vastness and inaccessibility make it difficult to extract most of these resources.

- **Sodium chloride**, better known as common salt, is one of the major minerals that are obtained from the oceans. It accounts for 3 percent of the weight of the ocean water.

- **Salt deposits** are formed when ocean water evaporates. Some lakes and rivers also contain salt deposits and crusts.

- **Other major minerals** obtained from the oceans are magnesium and bromine. Magnesium and its compounds are used in the agricultural, construction and chemical industries, while bromine is used in photography, and disinfectants.

- **Sedimentary rocks** such as limestone, sandstone and gypsum are also found in oceans. These are formed by erosion due to the action of water on shells and the remains of marine creatures. These are used in building materials.

- **Certain phosphorous minerals**, such as phosphorite, are also found on the seabed. These have potential uses as agricultural fertilizers.

- **Huge deposits** of manganese nodules have been recently discovered in the seabed, particularly in the Pacific Ocean. These nodules primarily consist of manganese and iron. Traces of copper, cobalt and nickel can also be found in them.

- **The oceans** are full of sulphur. Hydrothermal vents spout hot sulphur-rich water that also has a high concentration of other metals and minerals. Sulphur is used in fertilizers, food preservatives, bleaching agents and disinfectants.

- **Mining the oceans** is expensive and not very easy. There is an international dispute regarding the ownership of the oceans' mineral wealth.

- **An international maritime law** clearly defines the rules of sharing mineral wealth of the oceans. However, the debate continues on whether a particular spot in an ocean belongs to the nearest countries or to the global community.

Fossil fuels

- **Fossil fuels**, such as petroleum, coal and natural gas, are extracted from the fossilized remains of animals and plants that have been buried under layers of sediment, rocks and soil for millions of years.

- **Crude oil**, which is refined to make petroleum, is formed from microscopic plants and organisms such as bacteria that lived in the ancient oceans.

- **These micro-organisms** died and mixed with the silt in the ocean floor to form organic mud. Layers of sediment settled on this organic ooze, transforming it into crude oil.

- **Natural gas** is primarily formed by the decomposition or decaying of dead plankton that have accumulated on the ocean floor.

- **Both crude oil** and natural gas fill porous rocks nearby. These rocks containing reserves of fuel are called reservoir rocks. Since reservoir rocks are normally filled with water, the fuel, which is lighter than water, travels upwards until it reaches a layer of nonporous rocks.

- **The nonporous rocks** trap crude oil and natural gas to create a reservoir of fuel. Since natural gas is lighter than crude oil, it is found in a layer above the oil. Crude oil forms the middle layer with water as the bottom layer.

- **Coal** is a solid fossil fuel and is formed from decomposed plants that have hardened over the years. Coal is often found under the seabed, but offshore coal mining is not as widespread as that of oil and gas.

- **Scientists** have also found immense deposits of other hydrocarbon products, such as gas hydrates and oil shale, in the ocean floor.

- **Gas hydrates** are crystals of methane, while oil shale is a rock containing a waxy compound called kerogen.

- **Like crude oil**, oil shale is also formed from dead microscopic organisms. Over the years, these organisms are transformed into kerogen. However, the temperature and pressure in the ocean floor are sometimes not high enough to convert kerogen into crude oil.

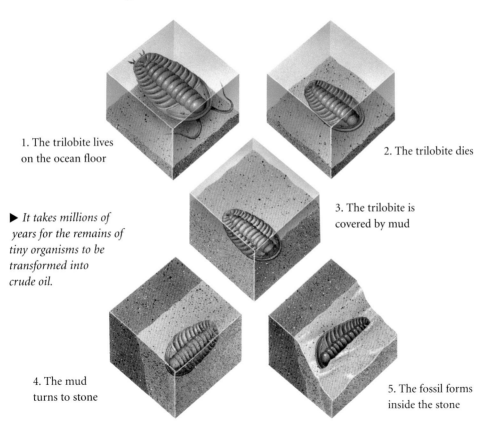

1. The trilobite lives on the ocean floor

2. The trilobite dies

3. The trilobite is covered by mud

▶ *It takes millions of years for the remains of tiny organisms to be transformed into crude oil.*

4. The mud turns to stone

5. The fossil forms inside the stone

189

Drilling for oil

- **With dwindling land resources**, the search for oil in the oceans is increasing. Natural resources found in the seabed are extracted and refined to produce fuel.

- **Oil companies** usually build offshore drilling rigs to extract resources from the seabed. Rigs are platforms set up in the sea at a distance from the shore.

- **Oil rigs** are tough structures made of steel or concrete that can withstand huge waves and storms. Alaskan oil rigs also have to withstand icy waters and ice floes.

- **These rigs** are equipped with massive, tubular drills that dig several hundred metres into the ocean floor. The samples brought up by these pipes are then tested for signs of crude oil.

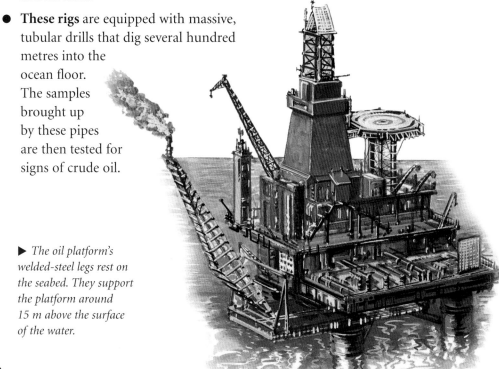

▶ *The oil platform's welded-steel legs rest on the seabed. They support the platform around 15 m above the surface of the water.*

- **Once the existence** of crude oil is confirmed, it is extracted and sent to refineries where it is refined into petroleum and petroleum products, such as kerosene.

- **Some oil rigs are huge platforms**, which drop an anchor and float on the water. These platforms have air-filled supports, and are called semi-submersible rigs.

- **Permanent oil rigs** are built in places where production is high and multiple oil wells can be drilled. Some of these rigs, measuring over 130 m in diameter and almost 245 m high, are held in place by concrete or steel legs.

- **Sometimes pressure** builds up in the underground wells, causing blow-outs. When a blow-out occurs the drilling hole explodes, spilling oil into the surrounding waters.

- **Mud, pipes and rocks** are also thrown into the air during a blow-out. Oil spills are harmful to the environment. Apart from polluting the water they also destroy marine life.

- **Blow-out preventers** control pressure in underwater wells while drilling.

> **. . . FASCINATING FACT . . .**
> Permanent oil rigs sometimes support an ecosystem.
> Their underwater structures form artificial reefs, with
> plenty of marine creatures living on them. Some
> offshore platforms are popular spots for rig diving.

Oil spills

▲ *Although oil tanker accidents, such as this, are considered to be most detrimental to marine life, they account for barely five percent of the total oil that flows into the oceans. The main oil pollutants are oil refineries and ships that wash their tanks at sea.*

- **Oil spills** are the worst form of ocean pollution. The effects of oil spills are long term and extremely damaging.

- **These are usually caused** when large ocean tankers have accidents while transporting their liquid cargo.

- **Oil does not mix** with water and so, during an oil spill, the oil spreads quickly, forming a thin, film-like layer on the surface, known as an 'oil slick'.

- **Oil also gets** into the oceans from pipelines and leaky, underground storage tanks. Heavier components of crude oil, such as polynuclear aromatic hydrocarbons, cause the most damage.

- **Oil slicks** are very harmful to marine life, as well as to birds and mammals living near the oceans. Oil damages the water-repellent properties in the fur of mammals like sea otters and the wings of birds.

- **Coral reefs**, mangroves and estuaries are very sensitive to oil spills.

- **The effects of oil spills** are not always immediate and the harm caused may be long-term. Oil spills often cause diseases of the liver and reproductive and growth problems in marine creatures.

- **The oil tanker** *Exxon Valdez* ran aground in 1989, dumping more than 38 million litres of oil into Prince William Sound, off the coast of Alaska. The damage caused was the worst in history.

- **The environmental damage** caused by the *Exxon Valdez* prompted the United States Congress to pass safety laws for oil tankers and barges. Oil companies were also made responsible for spill clean-up.

- **Another huge oil spill** was caused in 1978, by the American supertanker *Amoco Cadiz*, which ran aground off the coast of Brittany, France. The spill resulted in one of the largest ever losses of marine life.

Ocean pollution

- **People** have exploited oceans for their vast resources since ancient times. Excessive human activity in coastal areas has increased pollution and often caused irreparable damage to ocean life.

- **The discharge** of industrial waste and human sewage into the sea is the most common form of pollution. This affects marine creatures and makes the sea unfit for bathing.

- **The pollution** that enters oceans can be categorized as coming from 'point sources' and 'non-point sources'. Sewer pipes and industrial waste pipes are point sources, as the discharge is from a single, identifiable point.

- **Non-point sources** of pollution are more difficult to tackle. These include water or sewage from farms containing fertilizers with a high chemical content.

- **Some chemicals** found in pesticides, however, are biodegradable, and their effects are minimal and short-lived. Some remain dangerous for a long time.

- **Petroleum** and oil products are major pollutants that enter the water through spills from ships, and leakages from pipelines, tankers and storage tanks.

- **Power plants** are also a major source of pollution. The water discharged from power plants causes thermal pollution. The water is usually hot and so it alters the temperature of the sea water, affecting marine life adversely.

- **The numbers** of animals like dolphins, beluga whales, manatees, polar bears and other marine mammals have been diminished by industrial pollution and farm wastes.

- **Many beaches** have become tourist attractions. Plastic litter left on tourist beaches is a great hazard to marine life, proving fatal to some creatures.

● **Metals such as copper**, mercury, selenium and lead enter the oceans from industrial waste and automobile emissions. These can cause long-term health problems in both animals and humans.

▼ *Certain paints used to protect the hulls of ships and boats from barnacles contain poisonous chemicals and are fatal to marine creatures when discharged.*

Cleaning the oceans

- **People** are directly responsible for the dangers facing the oceans today. Our increasing demands have resulted in endangered marine animals, damaged ecosystems, melting ice caps and polluted seas.

- **The value** of the oceans' resources is now being recognized. Efforts are being made across the world to control the deterioration. Some nations are spending large amounts of money to protect the oceans.

- **The biggest problem** facing the oceans is global warming. Reducing the emission of greenhouse gases could stop global warming. Cleaner energy sources will control the release of carbon dioxide into the atmosphere.

- **The Kyoto Protocol**, a treaty aimed at reducing the release of greenhouse gases has been agreed upon by many nations. However, some of the largest polluting nations, such as the United States, have yet to sign it.

- **The harm caused** by synthetic chemicals and fertilizers that run off to the oceans, is being reversed by the use of eco-friendly chemicals. These chemicals are bio-degradable, which means that they decompose in a harmless way.

- **Chemical dispersants** break down oil into its chemical constituents, thus making it less harmful to the marine environment.

- **New devices** are being developed to absorb oil spills, which are one of the biggest threats to marine life. Heavier oil products often settle to the bottom, killing fragile, bottom-dwelling marine creatures.

- **Oil spills** are cleaned using booms, skimmers and chemical dispersants. On shore, low- or high-pressure water hoses and vacuum trucks are also used.

- **Floating barriers,** called 'booms', are placed around oil spills or their sources to prevent the oil from spreading further. Skimmers are boats with plastic ropes that skim over the surface, absorbing the oil after the booms have been set up.

- **To save coastlines**, many nations are imposing strict building regulations. Construction activity and tourism have damaged many coastal ecosystems.

▲ *Sorbents, or large sponges, are used in the final stages of a clean-up. These materials can absorb oil effectively, especially from beaches.*

Saving ocean life

▼ *These fish are proof of the horrors of chemical pollution. Thousands of dead marine creatures are washed ashore every year.*

- **Many marine species** have already become extinct, while several more are endangered.

- **Destruction of habitats**, pollution and overfishing are the main reasons for this. Efforts are being undertaken worldwide to save marine creatures.

- **Some ocean regions** are being specially protected. Fishing and other activities that disturb marine life in these areas are prohibited.

- **These regions** have been established as safe havens for endangered species and the protection of commercial fish stocks.

- **Only one percent** of the world's oceans, however, are protected. Many organizations, like the World Wildlife Fund, are trying to increase the coverage of protected areas.

- **Some habitats** are protected by the prohibition of destructive fishing gear. This ensures the development of the ecosystem, thus allowing fish species to grow to their normal size and produce more offspring.

- **The Great Barrier Reef** is one of the largest protected marine ecosystems. Commercial fishing and bleaching have destroyed vast stretches of these reefs.

- **Drilling for minerals**, oil or gas continues to pose a major threat to sensitive habitats. Efforts are being made to persuade companies to use methods that do not harm sea life.

- **Eco-tourism**, which brings people who are concerned about the environment to areas of natural beauty, helps fund conservation projects.

- **The population** of endangered marine species is being increased by many projects. Turtles, sharks and dolphins, for example, are being bred artificially under controlled conditions and then let out into the open seas.

Endangered species

- **Endangered species** are animals and plants that are facing extinction. These species will die out if nothing is done to keep them alive.

- **The main reasons** for a species becoming endangered are the destruction of their habitat by people, pollution and commercial exploitation by way of hunting and trade in animal parts such as elephant tusks.

- **Around 34,000 plant species** and 5200 animal species are close to extinction.

- **The current rate** of extinction is thought to be around 20,000 species every year. Studies suggest that this is the first age of mass extinction since the dinosaurs disappeared, nearly 65 million years ago.

- **When their habitats are destroyed**, many animals are not able to adapt quickly enough to the changed surroundings, which eventually leads to their extinction.

- **For marine life**, pollution and hunting are the major causes of extinction and endangerment. Excessive hunting has greatly reduced the numbers of sea turtles. Sea turtle eggs are a favourite food of both humans and animals.

- **Between the 1800s and the early 1900s**, whales were killed in large numbers for their meat and blubber. This led to the endangerment of many whale species.

- **Higher water temperatures**, along with pollution, have endangered several fish species. Oil spills kill many birds, fish and marine mammals.

- **Changes in biodiversity** can also lead to extinction. Biodiversity is where particular species thrive and depend on each other.

- **The kelp forest** in the North Pacific used to be one of the richest biodiversity zones. When humans killed sea otters in large numbers, the population of sea urchins, the main food of sea otters, increased. The sea urchins then ate more kelp, leading to the collapse of the entire ecosystem.

▼ *The sea otter is a protected species. This marine mammal was hunted in large numbers by humans because of its fur, which is the thickest in the animal kingdom.*

Whaling and fishing

- **Whaling** is the commercial hunting of whales for oil, meat, whalebone and other products. Whaling activity is believed to have begun in western Europe around the 900s.

- **In the 1100s**, whales were hunted off the coasts of Spain and Germany until their numbers were drastically depleted. Whaling in North America began with its colonization and was on an all-time high by the 1700s.

- **In the early 19th century**, whales were usually killed by harpoons and other weapons. Whaling became easier with the arrival of large boats, called 'factory ships', which were equipped with machinery to process slaughtered whales.

- **Sperm whales** were killed mainly for the type of oil that they produced, known as spermaceti. This was used as lubricants and in medicines.

- **The International Whaling Commission** was established in 1946, when whale populations began falling alarmingly. It regulated the hunting of whales, eventually leading to an increase in their numbers.

- **Fishing** is one of the biggest commercial activities carried out in the oceans. Fish are caught in large numbers to meet ever-growing demands. They are valuable protein sources.

> **...FASCINATING FACT...**
> Sport fishing, also called 'angling', is one of the most popular recreational activities in the world. Anglers use fishing rods and lines to catch game fish like marlin and swordfish.

202

▲ *Fishing trawlers are not only responsible for decreasing numbers of fish, but they also damage coral reefs. The heavy chains used to weigh down the nets often crush the reefs and kill enormous amounts of other marine creatures in the process.*

- **Mackerel,** herring and tuna are among the most caught and eaten fish around the world. Sharks are considered a delicacy in some parts of the world. Shellfish such as shrimps and lobsters are also popular.

- **Overfishing** has led to the endangerment of many fish species such as cod, mackerel and tuna.

- **The increasing world demand** for fish has led to the development of fish farms, where fish are grown and harvested for food.

- **Fish farming** provides about a fifth of all fish eaten – salmon, shrimp and carp are the most harvested. China leads the world in fish farming.

203

Crowding the coasts

▲ *Littering of beaches is one of the most common problems today. Tourists who visit coastal regions do not give much thought to the consequences of leaving behind debris.*

- **Coastal regions** are important for many reasons. The land along coasts is usually very fertile and therefore good for farming. The beaches also attract many tourists to coastal areas.

- **Since ancient times**, humans have made coastal areas their homes. Almost half of the world's population lives close to the coasts.

- **Most coastal regions** have, as a result, become overcrowded. This has led to pollution, damaged ecosystems and eroded coastlines.

- **People have built houses** and factories that discharge sewage and industrial waste into the seas. These damage the shores and pollute the oceans.

- **Industrial waste** contaminates bathing beaches and poisons shellfish beds. It also destroys natural habitats and has adverse affects on human health.

- **The development of ports**, roads, coastal construction, and mining of sand for construction material are destroying coastal habitats like coral reefs.

- **The shore** has also been damaged by attempts to control the movement of sediment such as sand and shingle. This prevents erosion in some places but leads to deposition of sediments in other areas.

- **Jetties and breakwaters** are built to protect harbour entrances and maintain a constant depth of water. These structures block the natural drift of sediment.

- **Artificial beaches** are built to reclaim land from the sea, thus damaging the coast beyond repair. Offshore dredging of sand to build beaches adds to the problem.

- **To attract tourists**, hotels and apartments are often built close to the water. This makes such areas vulnerable to pollution and disturbs the natural marine habitats and marine life.

Living at sea

- **Developers** are always thinking of new ways to make money from the popularity of islands and seas. Underwater hotels and artificial islands, such as the Jules' Undersea Lodge and the Palm Islands, are now capturing the imagination of people around the world.

- **The Jules' Undersea Lodge** in Florida, USA, is the world's first underwater hotel. Named after the French science-fiction writer Jules Verne, it was a research laboratory that was converted into a hotel for divers.

- **Visitors** have to dive over 6 m below the sea to enter the hotel through a 'moon pool' entrance in the floor of the hotel.

- **The Jules' Undersea Lodge** was first designed to be an underwater research laboratory called La Chalupa. Built in a mangrove lagoon, it was used to explore life in the continental shelf off the coast of Puerto Rico.

- **The world's first** underwater luxury hotel is being built off the coast of Dubai, in the United Arab Emirates. The Hydropolis Hotel will be built on the floor of the Persian Gulf, 20 m below the surface.

- **The hotel** will have three divisions. A land station will be the reception, while a connecting tunnel will transport guests from the land station into the depths of the ocean. A submarine complex will be the main hotel.

> ...FASCINATING FACT...
> The Jules' Undersea Lodge is filled with compressed air. This prevents the water from rising through the moon pool entrance and flooding the rooms.

▶ *Round glass windows that resemble huge portholes provide a wonderful view of the marine life at the Jules' Undersea Lodge.*

- **The Hydropolis** will also have two transparent domes that will hold an auditorium and a ballroom. The ballroom will be built above water, with a retractable roof.

- **The hotel** will be built of concrete, steel and clear Plexiglas that can withstand high underwater pressures.

- **The Palm Islands** in Dubai, popularly referred to as The Palm, are another oceanic wonder. They consist of two artificial islands in the shape of date palm trees.

- **Each palm island comprises** a trunk, a crown with 17 fronds and a crescent-shaped island forming an arch around them. The palm islands will accommodate luxury hotels, villas, apartments, restaurants and spas. The structures will increase Dubai's shoreline by 120 km.

207

Index

A

Aegean Sea 134, 135
Africa 11, 29, 95,
    108, 111, 118,
    120, 122, 128,
    129, 170, 173
aircraft carriers 142,
    149, 163,
    164–165, *164*
Abraham Lincoln
    165
assault carriers
    165
bombers 164
carrier battle
    group 165
fighters 164
fleet carriers 165
Fly, Eugene 165
HMS *Hibernia*
    165
light carriers 165
Samson, Charles
    165
steam-powered
    catapults 164
supercarriers 165
tailhooks 165
USS *Birmingham*
    165

Alaska 36, 92, 193
albatrosses **98–99**,
    98
wandering
    albatross 98
algae 30, 56, 78, 184
amphorae 139
ampullae of
    Lorenzini 65
ancient Greek navy
    112–113
bireme 112, 113,
    170
Byzantines 112
Graeco-Persian
    Wars 113
Greek Fire 112
penteconter 112
triremes *113*, 114
war galley 112
ancient Roman
    navy **114–115**,
    114
Carthage *114*
corvus 115
First Punic War
    114
gladiator battles
    115
quadriremes 114,
    115

quinqueremes
    114, 115
sprats 50
Antarctic Ocean 10,
    35, 38
International
    Hydrographic
    Organization 10
Southern Ocean
    10
Antarctica 10, 36,
    38–39, *39*, 41
Antarctic Treaty
    38
Greater
    Antarctica 38
nunatak 39
Ross Sea 38
sledges 37
snow petrels 39
South Pole 35, 38,
    103
Transantarctic
    Mountains 38, 39
Weddell Sea 38
West Antarctica
    38
Arabian Sea 121
Arctic Ocean 14, 10,
    11, 35, 36, 84
Siberian Shelf 14

Arctic region 35,
    36–37
Algonquian 37
Arctic Circle 36
Arctic fox 37
Arctic tundra 36
caribou 37
Eskimos 37
igloos 37
Inuktitut 37
Oymyakon 36
permafrost 36
snowmobiles *37*
tundra 36
tunturia 36
Argentina 124
artificial islands
    206, 207
Asia 11, 108, 110,
    118, 119, 122, 129
Atlantic Ocean 10,
    16, 30, 60, 117,
    118, 168, 169
Baltic Sea 10
Black Sea 10
Caribbean Sea 10,
    30, 33, 185
Denmark Strait
    10
Gulf of Mexico 10
Labrador Sea 10

Mediterranean Sea 10
Norwegian Sea 10
atoll **32–33**
lagoon 30, 32, 206
Australia 11, 29, 30, 33, **130–131**, 156, 173, 182
Botany Bay 131
Port Jackson 131
Sydney 131

B

Bahamas 118, 129
baleen whales 74, **75–76**, 82, 86
baleen plates 76, 79
great whales 75, 77, 80
whalebone 77, 202
Bangladesh 182
barnacles 195
barracuda **56–57**, *57*
great barracuda 56
basking sharks, filter feeders 76
battleships 142, **162–163**
Chih Yeun *162*

HMS *Devastation* 163
HMS *Thunderer* 163
line-of-battle ships 162
Missouri 163
Prince of Wales 163
bays 89, 156, 176
beaches 20, 27, 97, 177, 194, 197, 204, 205
Belize 33, 182
beluga whales 37, 74, **84–85**, *85*, 194
belukha 84
Delphinapterus leucas 84
melon 84
sea canaries 84
Bering Sea 35
Bermuda Triangle, Flight 15
Big Bang, collisions 8, 158
gases 9, 42, 177, 178, 180, 181, 196
helium 8
hydrogen 8, 9, 25

Bismarck 163
blowholes 74, 78, 86
blubber 37, 76, 77, 90, 201
blue sharks, mako 63
blue whales 75, **78–79**, *79*, 80
Brachiosaurus 78
bottom-dwelling sharks 65
Brazil 30, 122, 124, 164, 173, 190
Rio de Janeiro 122, 182

C

California, United States 22, 48, 92, 124,
Canada 29, 36, 52, 64, 67, 124, 157
British Columbia 157
cargo ships **110–111**, 142, 146
barge carrier 147
barges 147, 158, 193
box boats 147

bulk carriers 146, 147
cars 146, 147, 156
coasters 147
feeder vessels 147
freighters 146
food products 146
grain 117, 147
LASH 147
major ports 147
minor ports 147
ore 147
Phoenician trading ships 111
roll-on-roll-off 147
textiles 146
trucks 146, 147, 150, 196
wheeled containers 147
Caribbean Islands 95
Caribbean monk seal 91
Central America 119
chemical industries 187
chemicals 8, 13, 31, 142, 148, 194, 195, 196

Index

China 108, 170, 203
Chinese pirates 129
  junks 108, *109*,
  111
civilizations 11, 108,
  111
  Egyptian 11, 109,
  171
  Indus Valley 11,
  111
  Mesopotamian 11
clams 92
coast guards,
  helicopters 165
  lifeboats 161
coastal regions 56,
  204–205
  breakwaters 205
  debris 33, 204
  industrial waste
  194, 195, 205
  jetties 205
  littering *204*
  offshore dredging
  205
  overcrowded 205
  sewage 194, 205
  tourists 22, 204,
  205
coastline **20–21**
  artificial beaches
  205

beach heads 20
biodegradable 194
cliffs 20, 22, 97, 98
deposition 205
erosion 20, 21,
  187, 205
gravel 20, 22
headlands 20
Long Beach 20
mud 20, 188, 191
sand 20, 21, 22,
  33, 63, 72, 105,
  158, 205
sea arches 20, *21*
sea stacks 20, *21*
shingle 21, 205
cod 153, 203
coelacanth 42, *43*
  living fossils 43
Columbus,
  Christopher
  118–119
  Anjou, Africa 118
  Granada, Spain
  118
  King Ferdinand
  118
  Niña 118
  Palos, Spain 118
  Pinta 118
  Queen Isabella
  118

San Salvador 118
Santa Maria 118,
  119
Tunisia, Africa
  118
container ships 142,
  146, 147, **150–151**
containerization
  150
conveyor belts 150
cranes 147, 150,
  151
derricks 147
docks 147, 158
electric fork-lift
  trucks 150
fruit 142, 150
Ideal X 150
Mclean, Malcolm
  150
Port Elizabeth,
  New Jersey,
  United States 150
reefers 142, 150,
  151
refrigerated ships
  150
Shenzhen 150
Cook, James
  130–131
  Endeavour 130
  coracles 108

coral reefs **30–31**,
  32, 33, 58, 61,
  182, 183, 184,
  185, 193, 203,
  205
  barrier reefs 30
  barrier reef
  islands 32
  bleaching
  184–185, 187, 199
  cays 33
  Christmas Island
  33
  coral atolls 33, 30,
  182
  coral polyps 30,
  184
  Coral Sea Islands
  33
  Easter Island 185
  fringing reefs 30
  Glover's Reef 33
  hard corals 185
  Kiribati Islands 33
  Lighthouse Reef
  33
  Line Islands 33
  Marshall 33
  non-reef building
  corals 185
  Republic of
  Kiribati 33

soft corals *185*
Sri Lanka 185
Tanzania 185
Tuamotu 33
Turneffe Atoll 33
zooxanthellae 184
Coral Sea 33, 30
corals 30, **32–33**, 42,
 184, 185
crabs 30, 52, 60, 64,
 73, 91, 105
crustaceans 73, 101
Cuba 118
cuttlefish 98

D

Denmark 10, 116
denticles 62, 64
dermal denticles 62
destroyers 142
Dias, Bartolomeu
 120
diving equipment
 138
diving suits
 140–141
 aqualung *141*
 Klingert's diving
 suit 140
 portable air
 supply system 141

Siebe, August 140
visors 140
weight belt 140
dolphins 45, 74, 80,
 84, **86–87**, 88,
 94, 194, 199
 bottlenose
 dolphins 86, *87*
 echolocation 74,
 86
 tucuxi dolphin 86
Dominican
 Republic 118
dorsal fins 56
Drake, Sir Francis
 124–125, 126, 129
 Celebes 125
 Golden Hind 124,
 125
 Guam 123
 Isthmus of
 Panama 124
 Java 125, 130
 Queen Elizabeth I
 124, 125
 Rio de la Plata
 124
dreadnoughts 163
dredgers 160, 158
Dubai, UAE 206,
 207

Hydropolis Hotel
 206
 retractable roof
 207
dugouts 108

E

eared seals 90, 92
Earth **8–9**, 10, 12,
 13, 14, 16, 18,
 19, 24, 36, 38,
 42, 122, 136,
 137, 145, 178,
 180, 181
 acids 8
 atmosphere 8, 9,
 13, 42, 74, 177,
 180, 181, 196
 axis 36
 continents 11, 14,
 38
 core 8
 crust 8, 9, 16, 24,
 13
 mantle 8, 26
 nitrogen 9, 184
 Northern
 Hemisphere 18
 oxygen 8, 53, 90,
 107

planet 8, 14, 32,
 74, 78, 105, 181
 radioactive
 elements 8
 rotation 18
 salts 8
 silicon 8
 Southern
 Hemisphere 18,
 98
 tectonic plates 8,
 16, 24, 26, 13
 volcanic activity *9*,
 24, 26
ecosystem 32, 191,
 184, 199, 201
ecosystems 12, 45,
 199, 196, 197, 205
eels 30, **58–59**, *59*,
 107
 American eel 58
 conger eel **58–59**
 elvers 58
 european eel *59*
 freshwater eels 58
 green moray *59*
 gulper eels 58
 moray eels 58
 snake eel *59*
Egypt 108, 110
El Niño 28, 29, *177*,
 178

Index

endangered species 79, 199, **200–201**
  biodiversity zones 201
  extinction 201
  factories 205
  fish species 47, 199, 201, 203
  fish stocks 199
  fishing gear 143, 199
  harbour entrances 205
  hunting 50, 79, 91, 92, 93, 100, 201, 202
  kelp forest 201
  lead 26, 56, 65, 121, 137, 149, 177, 181, 195, 201
  lubricants 202
  mangroves 193
  mass extinction 201
  overfishing 55, 180, 199, 203
  pollution 180, 194, 193, 198, 199, 201, 205
England 124, 125, 126, 127, 131, 132, 135

English Channel 156
environment 148, 149, 151, 177, 180, 190, 191, 197, 199
enzymes 42
Erik the Red, Newfoundland 135
estuaries 89, 193
Europe 129, 134, 155, 156, 170, 202

F

fauna 13
ferries **156–157**, *157*
  apron 156
  Bass Strait 156
  hydrofoils 156
  Puget Sound 157
  Spirit of Tasmania 156
  Staten Island Ferry 156, 157
  Strait of Georgia 157
  waterbus 156
fertilizers 187, 194, 196

films,
  Cameron, James 134
  Jaws 54, 60, 74, 86
fishing 47, 57, 64, 87, 92, 100, 108, 143, 152, 153, 171, 174, 199, 202, 203
  angling 202
  fish farming 203
  fish farms 203
  harvested 203
fishing vessels **152–153**
  bycatch 153
  dive boats 153
  draggers 152
  drag heavy nets 152
  fishermen 28, 152
  fishing nets 87, 92, 153
  head boats 153
  long-liners 153
  lobster boats 143
  lobsters boats 153
  seiner nets 153
  seiners 143, 152, 153
  trawlers 143, 152, *153*, 203

  trawls 152, 153
flatworms 42
flippers 82, 86, 90, 92, 103, 105
flora 13
Florida, United States 30, 94, 182, 206, 207
flukes 74
flying fish **48–49**, *49*
  California flying fish 48
fossil fuels **188–189**
  bacteria 188
  coal 147, 188
  crude oil 142, 149, 188, *189*, 191, 193
  decomposed 188
  gas hydrates 188
  hydrocarbon 188
  kerogen 188, 189
  methane 188, 180
  natural gas 14, 188, 148
  nonporous rocks 188
  oil shale 188, 189
  organic ooze 188
  porous rocks 188
  reservoir rocks 188

France 127, 132, 155, 164, 193
frigates 142, *143*
  anti-submarine warfare 143

G

Galapagos fur seals 90
Galapagos Islands 25, 92, 103
  ALVIN 25
  tubeworms *25*
galleys 112, 170
Gama, Vasco da **120–121**, *121*
  Calicut 121
  Cochin 121
  Estevão da Gama 120
  Goncalo Alvares 120
  King João II 120
  Malindi 121
  Mombassa 121
  Mozambique 121
  Nicolao Coelho 120
  Paolo da Gama 120
Germany 202

gill slits 71
glaciers **40–41**, 177, 178, 181, 182
  Alpine glaciers 41
  continental glaciers 40, 41
  continuous snowfall 40
  ice sheets 35, 41, 144, 158
  icecap glaciers 41
  Piedmont glaciers 41
Golden Age of Piracy **128–129**, *128*
  island of Nassau 129
  plutarch 128
Great Barrier Reef 30, 31, 182, *183*, 185, 199
  hydroid coral 31
  Red Sea 30
Great Britain 52, 64, 156
great white sharks 64, **66–67**, *67*
  breaching 66, 77
  white death 66
  white pointer 66
Greece 113

green sea turtles 104
greenhouse effect, 178, **180–181**, *181*
  Antarctic ice packs 182
  carbon dioxide 177, 180, 181, 196
  chlorofluorocarbons 180
  deforestation 181
  enhanced greenhouse effect 178, 180
  Everglades, Florida, United States 182
  flooding 177, 182, 206
  global warming 177, 178, 180, 181, 182, 184, 196
  greenhouse 177, 178, 180, 181, 196
  greenhouse gases 177, 178, 180, 181, 196
  Kyoto Protocol 177, 196
  Maldives 182, 185
  greenhouse effect 180
  nitrous oxide 180

ozone 180
polar ice caps 177, 181
sea level 16, 177, 182
Seychelles 182
temperature 13, 18, 25, 36, 38, 47, 53, 77, 140, 177, 178, 184, 189, 194
Tuvalu 182
water vapour 9, 180
Greenland 36, 37, 41, 108, 177
Greenland sharks 37
grey whales 75
guffa 110
gulls **96–97**, *96*, 98
  black-headed gulls 97
  great black-backed gull 97
  plumage 96, 97
  ring-billed gulls 97

H

habitats 47, 199, 201, 205

Index

Haiti 118, 119
hammerhead sharks **68–69**
  bonnethead sharks 69
  great hammerhead *68*, 69
  scalloped hammerhead 69
  smooth hammerhead 69
  stingrays 69
hatchet fish 45
Hawaii 24, 27, 173
herring 54, **50–51**, *51*, 97, 153, 202
  anchovies 50, 56, 71
  Atlantic herring 50, 51
  bloaters 51
  dried 51
  kippers 51
  menhaden 50
  Pacific herring 51
  pickled 51
  pilchard 50
  red herring 50, 51
  sardines 50, 71
  Sardinia 50
  shad 50
  smoked 50, 51
  wolf herring 51
hull 117, 134, 135, 149, 156, 170, 174
humpback whales 75, *76*, 77, **82–83**, *83*
  bubble-netting 82
  lunge-feeding 82
  tail-flicking 82
  tubercles 82, 89
hurricanes 28
  category 5 28
  cyclones 28
  typhoons 28

I

ice shelves 35, 41
  Ross Ice Shelf 35
icebergs 35, **40–41**, *40*, 84
iceboats 142
icebreakers 160, **161–162**
Iceland 16, 27, 36, 117
India 120, 121, 170, 164, 182
Indian Ocean 11, 30, 185
Inuit 35, 37, 108
Ireland 127, 134
island arcs 27
Italy 22, 156, 164

J

Jamaica 119
Japan 28
Jason and the Argonauts, dragon 117
jawed fish 47
  bony fish 42, 47, 62, 72
  cartilage 47, 72
  cartilaginous fish 47, 72
  chimeras 47
jawless fish 42, 47
  lamprey 42, 47
  hagfish 42, 47
jellyfish 30, 35, 42, 105
jet boats 142
jet skis **176–177**, *176*
  ballets 177
  gymnasts 177
  human pyramids 177
  long skis 177

personal watercraft 176, 177
skiers 176, 177
skiing 174, 176, 177

K

kalakku 110
Kamchatka 35
keel 117, 170
Kenya 121, 185
killer whales 74, **80–81**, *81*, 85, 91, 92
  demon dolphin 80
  Dephinus orca 80
  orcas 37, 80
  resident pods 80
  transient pods 80, 81
Kiritimati 33

L

Labrador Sea 10
lakes 9, 187, 176
larvae 58
lateral line 65
leopard seals 91, 103
Lisbon, Portugal 120

214

lobsters 30, 153, 202
lobtailing 77
logging 77
London, England 182
Los Angeles, United States 182
low-lying areas 182

M

mackerel 48, **52–53**, 54, 64, 202, 203
  Atlantic mackerel 52, 64
  chub mackerel 52, 64
  food poisoning 52
  Scombridae 52
Magellan, Ferdinand 10, **122–123**, *122*
  Cano, Sebastian del 123
  circumnavigate 123
  King Charles I 122
  Magellan's Strait 123
  Moluccas 123, 125

Spice Islands 122, 123
Strait of All Saints 123
Tierra del Fuego 123, 124
marine biology 12
  Aristotle 138
marlin 54, 202
  game fish 202
  sailfish 47, 54
melting 178, 177, 181, 182, 196
mermaids 95
  sirens 95
Mexico 10, 33
minerals 13, 14, 25, 30, 146, 186, 187, 199
  bromine 187
  cobalt 187
  copper 140, 187, 195
  gypsum 187
  iron 8, 117, 136, 142, 187
  limestone 186, 187
  magnesium 187
  manganese 187
  manganese nodules 187

metals 146, 187, 195
  nickel 8, 187
  phosphorite 187
  phosphorous 187
  salt 13, 18, 107, 187
  sandstone 187
  sodium chloride 187
  sulphur 187
minesweepers 153
mining 187, 188, 205
modern fish 44
  neopterygians 44
molluscs 42
motorboats 37, 142, **174–175**
  high-speed boats 174, 175
  hydroplanes 174
  inboard motors 174
  internal combustion engines 174
  offshore powerboat racing 175
  outboard motors 174

powerboat racing *175*
runabouts 174
sponsons 174
tunnel boats 174
water-jet engine 174

N

Napoleon **132–133**
  Cadiz 133, 193
  Cape Trafalgar 133
  Villeneuve, Charles de 132
nasal barbels 65
natural resources 148, 190
naval convoy, escort carriers 165
navigation 13, 136, 137, **144–145**
  dead reckoning 137
  GPS *144*, 145
  jackstaff 137
  knots 136, 163
  lodestone 136
  Loran 145
  magnetic compass 136

Index

mariner's compass 136
Morse Code 145
nautical charts 137
radar 144, 145
radio direction finding 144, 145
sextant 136, 137
Nelson **132–133**, *133*
British Mediterranean fleet 132
Toulon 132
New York, United States 135, 156, 182
New Zealand 130
Aborigines 130, 131
Dampier, William 130
Hartog, Dirk 130
Jansz, Willem 130
Nieu Zelandt 130
Phillip, Captain Arthur 131
nictitating membrane 65
Nile 108, 110
North Africa 128

North America 92, 202
North Pole 10, 35, 36
northern fur seals, Okhotsk Sea 35
Northern Ireland 134
United States 157
Norway 29, 52, 64, 116

O

ocean floor 13, **14–15**, *15*, 16, 24, 25, 29, 45, 58, 188, 189, 191
abyssal plains 14
canyons 14, 16
continental margin 14
continental rise 14
continental shelf 14, 206
continental slope 14
deep valleys 16
mid-ocean ridges 15
ocean pollution 193, **194–195**, *195*

automobile emissions 195
farm wastes 194
industrial pollution 194
non-point sources 194
pesticides 194
plastic litter 194
point sources 194
power plants 194
sewer pipes 194
selenium 195
storage tanks 193, 194
thermal pollution 194
oceanography **12–13**
chemical marine geology 12, 13
hydrography 13
marine geologists 13
marine science 12
meteorological oceanography 12, 13
oceanology 12
physical oceanography 12, 13

satellite photograph *12*
speleology 13
octopus 45, 92
shellfish 91, 202, 205
oil rigs 158, 160, **190–191**, *190*
Alaskan oil rigs 190
artificial reefs 191
blow-out preventers 191
blow-outs 191
ice floes 190
kerosene 191
offshore oil rig 190
offshore drilling rigs 190
oil wells 191
oil companies 190, 193
Petrobas 28, 190
refineries 191, 192
rig diving 191
semi-submersible rigs 191
oil spills 148, 180, 191, **192–193**, 196, 201
Amoco Cadiz 193

bio-degradable
196
booms 196
Brittany 193
chemical
dispersants 196,
197
Exxon Valdez 193
oil slick 193
oil tanker 192, 193
oil tanker
accidents *192*
polynuclear
aromatic
hydrocarbons 193
pipelines 148, 149,
194, 193
Prince William
sound 193

P

Pacific Ocean 10,
11, 15, 16, 24,
25, 26, 27, 28,
29, 33, 48, 52,
56, 58, 64, 89,
92, 122, 123,
124, 125, 130,
169, 178, 182, 187
Mount Everest 11,
16, 24

pacifico 10
mucus 58
passenger ships 142,
154–155
Britannic 134, 135
cruise ships 154
Cunard Line 155
Cunard, Samuel
155
Freedom Ship 154
Lusitania 155
Mauretania 155
Normandie 155
ocean liners 154,
155
Olympic 134, 135
Olympic-class
liners 134, 135
Queen Mary 155
Queen Elizabeth 2,
155
White Star Line
134, 155
pectoral fins 48, 73
glide 48, 98
pelagic zone 45
benthic zone 45
epipelagic zone 45
midnight zone 45
twilight zone 45
pelicans **100–101**,
101

American white
pelicans 100
brown pelican 100
Peruvian pelicans
100
pelvic fins 48, 54
penguins 91,
102–103, *102*
Adélie penguins
103
fairy penguin 103
little blue penguin
103
rockhopper
penguins 103
perishable goods
142
Perseus,
Greek mythology
95
Persian Gulf 206
Palm Islands 206,
207
petrels 39
petroleum 14, 142,
146, 148, 188,
191, 194
Philippines 16, 123
Phoenicians 109,
110, 112, 170
pinnipeds 90

Pirates,
Nassau 129
privateering 129
pirate ships 129
captain 95, 130,
131
cook 130
Pirate torture,
marooning 128
Pirate treasure,
spices 121, 123
plankton 31, 45, 50,
60,62, 71, 73, 76,
78, 184, 188
pods 77, 80, 81
polar bears 35, 37,
45, 85, 91, 194
Polar life,
lichens 36
mosses 36
shrubs 36
wolf 51
polar regions 35, 40,
158, 177
porpoises 74, **88–89**
Burmeister's
porpoises 89
Dall's porpoises
89
dalli 89
harbour porpoises
88, 89

Index

rooster-tail splash 89
spectacled porpoises 89
spinipinnis 89
spray porpoise 89
truei 89
Portugal 13, 118, 120, 124, 126, 170
predators 48, 49, 56, 60, 62, 91, 105
privateers 129
Puerto Rico 206

R

rafts 108, 109, 110
rays 45, 46, 47, 66, **72–73**
electric ray 73
manta rays *46*, 73
ratfish 72
spotted eagle ray *72*
stingray 73
reef sharks 30, 62
ridges 15, 16, 33
right whales 75
ringed seals 90
rivers 9, 21, 41, 58, 84, 109, 110, 156, 158, 176, 187

rowing boats **168–169**
canoe polo 169
canoes 168, 169
carbon fibre 169
coxless 169
coxswain 169
double-ended paddles 169
fibreglass 142, 169, 174, 176
kayaks 37, 108, 169
outriggers 169
Polynesian peoples 169
rowing boats, rodeo canoeing 169
sculling 169
slalom canoeing 169
sweeping 169

S

sailboats 142, 168, 170, 171
sailing ships 112, **170–171**
caravels 170
cogs 170

rudders 108, 170
oarsmen 117, 112, 113, 115, 170
fellucas 171
galleons 170
gunwale 170
masts 170
Mayflower 170
salmon 84, 100, 152, 203
schools 48, 50, 51, 52, 53, 54, 56, 64, 71, 108
Scotland 127
scuba **140–141**, *141*
scuba diving 140
dry suits 140
Fleuss, Henry 141
rebreather 141
wet suits 140
scurvy 123
sea anemones 22
sea caves 20, **22–23**, *23*
Blue Grotto 22
Capri, Italy 22
Painted Cave 22
Santa Cruz Island 22
sea cows **94–95**
Bering, Captain Vitus 95

dugongs 94, 95
manatees 94, 95, 194
sirenians 95
sea lions 66, 90, **92–93**, *93*
Steller's sea lions 92
sea otters 193, *200*, 201
sea snakes 105, **106–107**
aquatic sea snakes 107
sea kraits 107
viviparous 107
yellow-bellied sea snake 107
sea stacks *21*
sea turtles 66, **104–105**, 201
sea urchins 201
seabirds 35, 45, 50, 80, 97, 99, 105
seahorses **60–61**, *61*
common seahorse 60
pipefish 60
sea moths 60
seadragons 60
shrimpfish 60
trumpetfish 60
seaweeds 60

pouch 60, 100
ships **142–143**
shipbuilding 109, 110
Queen Elizabeth 124, 125, 155
shrimps 73, 82, 202
krill 71, 73, 76, 78, 82, 103
Siberia 36
Singapore 182
snouts 65
Solar System 8
South Africa 173
South America 28, 29, 89, 122, 177
southern elephant seal 90
Spain 13, 118, 119, 122, 123, 124, 126, 132, 133, 164, 170, 202
Spanish Armada **126–127**, *126*, 170
Battle of Gravelines 127
Cádiz 126
Calais 127
Howard, Lord Charles 127
marqués de Santa Cruz 126

Medina-Sidonia 126
Naples, Italy 126
Philip II 126
Plymouth 127
sperm whales *74*, 202
medicines 60, 151, 202
spined pygmy shark 62
sponges 22, 30, 42, 105, 197
sport fishing 202
spyhopping 77
squid 35, 45, 56, 69, 74, 80, 84, 91, 92, 98
starfish 22, 30
stars 136
stern 108, 111, 117, 129, 147, 135, 169, 170, 174
streams 9, 47
sub-tropical 28, 104
submarines 161, **166–167**, *167*
American War of Independence 166
attack submarines 167
ballast tanks 166

ballistic missile submarines 167
Bushnell, David 166
Drebbel, Cornelius Jacobszoon 166
hunter-killer submarines 167
nuclear-powered submarines 166
periscopes 166
torpedoes 166, 167
turtle 104, 105, 166, 201
submersibles **160–161**
Nautile 160
Sun 18, 19, 36, 103, 136, 137, 180, 181
Mercury 195
Moon 18, 19, 206
surfing **172–173**, 177
aerials 173
board sailing 172
longboards 173
shortboards 173
skateboarding 173
surfboard 172, 173

surfers 67, 173
snowboarding 173
swordfish **54–55**, *55*, 202
game fishing 57
sword 54

T

tail fin 58, 66, 78, 82
tankers 142, 146, **148–149**, *148*, 158, 193, 194
Liquid Natural Gas 148
Medium Range Carriers 148
PANAMAX 148
Seawise Giant 149
SUEZMAX 148
supertankers 146, 149
TT Jahre Viking 149
Ultra Large Crude Carriers 148
Very Large Crude Carriers 148
Tasman, Abel 130
Tasmania 130, 156
temperate 50, 54, 66, 69, 71, 80

Index

tenders **160–161**, 165
  dinghies 161
  lifeboat tenders 161
  submarine tenders 161
tentacles 30
Thailand 164
tide 19
tiger sharks 62
Titanic **134–135**, *135*, 155, 160
  Astor IV, John Jacob 135
  Californian 135
  Carpathia 135
  Futrelle, Jacque 135
  Guggenheim, Benjamin 135
  HMS *Hawke* 135
  Jessup, Violet Constance 135
  Millet, Francis Davis 135
  Royal Mail steamer 134
  Southampton 135
  transatlantic liners 134

toothed whales 74, 77, 84, 86, 88
trenches 15, **16–17**, Challenger Deep 16, 17
  Mariana Trench 15, 16
  mid-Atlantic ocean ridge 16
  Piccard, Jacques 17
  seamount 16, 27
  Trieste 17
  Walsh, Don 17
trilobites *189*
Trinidad and Tobago 119
tropical 28, 54, 56, 69, 71, 82, 95, 104
true seals 90, 92
tsunamis 28
  Awa 28
  earthquakes 13, 28
  harbour wave 28
  landslides 28
  tidal waves 28
tube worms *25*
tugboats **158–159**, *159*, 160
  harbour tugs 158
  long-haul tugs 158

ocean-going tugs 158
  short-haul tugs 158
  tugs 158
tuna 48, **52–53**, *53*, 153, 202, 203
  bluefin tuna 53
  canned 50, 53
  chicken of the sea 53

U

undersea diving 33
undersea volcanoes **24–25**, 26
  benthic worms 25
  black smokers 25
  fissures 26
  giant tube worms 25
  guyots 24
  hot springs 24
  hydrothermal vents 24, *25*, 187
  Jericho worms 25
  magma 24, 26, 27
  Mauna Kea 24, 26, 27
  Mauna Loa 24, 26, 27

orange worms 25
  pillow lava 24
  Ring of Fire 24, 28
  seamounts 16, 24, 26
  undersea volcanic eruptions 28
underwater diving, Cousteau, Jacques 141
  Gagnan, Emile 141
underwater explorers **138–139**, *139*
  Alexander the Great 138, 139
  diving bell 138, 139
  kalimboi 139
  Madrague de Giens 139
  Peloponnesian Wars 138
  Scione 138
  Sparta 138
  Syracuse 138
  Thucydides 138
  Tyre 139
  urinatores 139
underwater hotels **206–207**

compressed air 206, 166
Jules' Undersea Lodge 206, *207*
La Chalupa 206
moon pool 206
United Arab Emirates 206
United Kingdom 38, 164
United States 20, 22, 29, 30, 50, 52, 64, 95, 124, 134, 135, 155, 164, 165, 173, 182, 193, 196, 206

V

Venezuela 119
Venice 156
Verne, Jules 206
vertebrates 47
Vespucci, Amerigo, Americas 118, 122, 124, 125, 129
King Manuel I 120
New World 122
Vietnam 182
Vikings **109–116**, 117, 170

dragon ships 117
knarr 116
knórr 116, 117
longship 116, 117, 170
Norse 116
viperfish 45
bioluminescent 45
photophores 45
volcanic islands 24, 26, 27, 33
Aleutian Islands 27
Big Island 26
Hawaiian Islands 26
hot spots 26
Hualalai 26
Kilauea 26
Kohala 26
Marianas 27
oceanic high islands 26
volcanoes 9, 13, 16, 24, 26, 27

W

Wales 163
walruses 90
warships 112, 114, 142, 143, 164, 166, 167

Washington 20, 157
water skiing 174, 176
jet skis 177
jump event 177
Kawasaki Heavy Industries 176
Lake City 176
Lake Pepin 176
Minnesota 176
Ralph Samuelson 176
rubber mouldings 176
show skiing 177
slalom event 176
trick skiing 177
wakeboarding 177
water sports 177
waves **18–19**, 20, 21, 22, 28, 32, 33, 74, 86, 145, 169, 173, 176, 177, 190
gravitational pull 18
breaker 18
Coriolis Effect 18
currents 13, 18, 20, 29, 55, 65, 110, 168
gyres 18

high tide 18, 19, 22
low tide 18, 19
neap tides 19
spring tides 19
tides 13, 18, 19, 29
whale sharks **70–71**
fish eggs 71, 107
whaling 108, **202–203**
anglers 57, 202
factory ships 202
harpoons 202
International Whaling Commission 202
regulated 202
spermaceti 202
whirlpools 28, 29
Moskstraumen 29
Deer Island 29
Old Sow 29
women pirates, solar heat 178
World War I 155, 163, 166
seaplane tenders 165
World War II 155, 163, 166
dockyards 158
Yamato 163

World Wildlife
  Fund 199
  commercial
  fishing 152, 199
  conservation 199
  eco-friendly
  chemicals 196
  eco-tourism 199
  prohibition 199
  protected areas
    199
  skimmers 196
  sorbents 197
  vacuum trucks
    196
wreck diving,
  salvage operations
    161, 174
  wreck divers 161

Z

zooplankton 30, 47

Acknowledgements

All artworks are from Miles Kelly Artwork Bank

The Publishers would like to thank the following picture source
whose photograph appears in this book:

Page 207 Stephen Frink/CORBIS

All other photographs from:

Castrol, CMCD, Corbis, Corel, digitalSTOCK, digitalvision
Flat Earth, Hemera, ILN, John Foxx, PhotoAlto, PhotoDisc
PhotoEssentials, PhotoPro, Stockbyte